Icelandic Pop

The REVERB series looks at the connections between music, artists and performers, musical cultures and places. It explores how our cultural and historical understanding of times and places may help us to appreciate a wide variety of music, and vice versa.

reverb-series.co.uk
SERIES EDITOR: JOHN SCANLAN

Already published

The Beatles in Hamburg
IAN INGLIS

Brazilian Jive: From Samba to Bossa and Rap
DAVID TREECE

Crooner: Singing from the Heart from Sinatra to Nas
ALEX COLES

Easy Riders, Rolling Stones: On the Road in America, from Delta Blues to '70s Rock
JOHN SCANLAN

Five Years Ahead of My Time: Garage Rock from the 1950s to the Present
SETH BOVEY

Gypsy Music: The Balkans and Beyond
ALAN ASHTON-SMITH

Heroes: David Bowie and Berlin
TOBIAS RÜTHER

Icelandic Pop: Then, Today, Tomorrow, Next Week
ARNAR EGGERT THORODDSEN

Jimi Hendrix: Soundscapes
MARIE-PAULE MACDONALD

The Kinks: Songs of the Semi-Detached
MARK DOYLE

The Monkees: Made in Hollywood
TOM KEMPER

Neil Young: American Traveller
MARTIN HALLIWELL

Nick Drake: Dreaming England
NATHAN WISEMAN-TROWSE

Peter Gabriel: Global Citizen
PAUL HEGARTY

Remixology: Tracing the Dub Diaspora
PAUL SULLIVAN

Song Noir: Tom Waits and the Spirit of Los Angeles
ALEX HARVEY

Sting: From Northern Skies to Fields of Gold
PAUL CARR

Tango: Sex and Rhythm of the City
MIKE GONZALEZ AND MARIANELLA YANES

Transatlantic Drift: The Ebb and Flow of Dance Music
KATIE MILESTONE AND SIMON A. MORRISON

Van Halen: Exuberant California, Zen Rock'n'roll
JOHN SCANLAN

Icelandic Pop

Then, Today, Tomorrow, Next Week

Arnar Eggert Thoroddsen

REAKTION BOOKS

I dedicate this book to Móheiður, Ísold, Karólína, Coco, Máni, Sushi, Mandla, Mysingur, Árni and Simon. Hearty thanks to my friend Dr. Gunni for manuscript reading and valuable pointers.

Published by Reaktion Books Ltd
2–4 Sebastian Street
London EC1V 0HE, UK
www.reaktionbooks.co.uk

First published 2025

EU GPSR Authorised Representative
Logos Europe, 9 rue Nicolas Poussin, 17000, La Rochelle, France
email: contact@logoseurope.eu

Printed and bound in Great Britain by Bell & Bain, Glasgow

A catalogue record for this book is available from the British Library

ISBN 978 1 83639 114 2

Contents

Preface

When I was asked to write this book, one of the requests was to 'explain the phenomenon', the phenomenon being the Icelandic popular music scene. This request adheres to the notion that something special is going on in Iceland musically, something out of the ordinary, something that is often said to be out of sync with its small population. To put it another way: why is there so much music – and so much quality music – coming from such a small country? The cultural sociologist Nick Prior writes, in his fine excursion into the music life of Iceland's capital, 'with a population of only 120,000, Reykjavík, in particular, has been lauded as a hub of prodigious musical activity, its status enhanced by associations with a spirit of frenetic creativity.'[1]

We, the locals, can't help but shake our heads when we face some of these excited proclamations – and perhaps even smirk about them. The enthusiasm is sometimes excessive, and unfounded opinions on Iceland's music scene are widely publicized, often underscored with a sense of exoticism. Writings and discussions relating to the 'phenomenon' tend to be simplified and exaggerated, especially when declarations about Iceland's 'unique' music scene are put in a per capita context. Both the foreign media and Icelanders themselves have a tendency to opt for chest-beating statements about the unbelievable greatness of the music scene, rather than a sober look at the realities of the country's music culture.[2] People's attachment to a particular romanticized view of the nation tempts many a music enthusiast to perpetuate dubious, subjective ideals and images that fit to what they want to see – and hear – in Iceland.[3] Interest in the 'mundane' truth is thus diminished, the rose-tinted glasses always within reach, and the everyday reality of music-making in Iceland is overlooked – both in newspaper headlines and research projects.

At the same time, all of this gets to you as an Icelander. There must be some truth to all of these claims – or what? Yes, we have musicians who are quite good. Yes, some of them have been making waves abroad. But is it something quite unique and special, compared to other nations? Or rather, compared to other small nations? What can we attest to and what can we deny in all of this? Jamaica is a small nation but with an immense influence on world music culture, introducing it to reggae. Still, the population is a little under 3 million, much higher than in Iceland (a little over 400,000 at the time of publication). The dynamics of Iceland's music culture and the all-around proximity is more akin to a city like Glasgow, even if that city's population is much higher (the metro area has 1.8 million people). But again, this is a misleading comparison, as Glasgow is a single city in a nation of millions, while Iceland is an independent nation with its own comprehensive infrastructure.

Popular music culture – that is, the Anglo-American pop/rock variety – reached these shores a little after the advent of American rock 'n' roll. In the aftermath of the Second World War, the country – an underdeveloped society under Danish colonial rule well into the twentieth century – saw swift social and economic progress. Iceland became an independent nation in 1944, and in the subsequent decades of popular music-making the country aligned itself with other Scandinavian countries in emulating the most recent trends of Anglo-American pop and rock. For decades the music managed to demand only domestic interest, most of it non-exportable. Regular efforts were made to entice interest from abroad to no avail.

The much-heralded underground rock band The Sugarcubes, later giving rise to superstar Björk, changed all of that in 1988, snowballing an interest in Icelandic popular music 'radically disproportionate to its size'.[4] This interest has grown steadily since, gradually shifting from mere curiosity in the quirks of Björk and the mystical grandeur of Sigur Rós to an all-encompassing fascination with Icelandic popular music in general. People – music enthusiasts, academics and even those with a passing interest in music – are genuinely curious about how a small Nordic nation with a population of 400,000 manages to nurture varied, active music scenes with a distinctive creative output that attracts worldwide attention. This has in turn led to and fuelled a more general interest in the country as such, its landscape, history, social structure and so forth. The question then beckons: what are the connections between the music and the place it emerges from?

In the following chapters I will attempt to shed a light on these matters. To that aim, and to fully understand how Iceland reached this position, we need to look at the big picture – that is, nothing less than Iceland's popular music history. I will trace that history by devoting a chapter to each decade, beginning with the 1950s and ending in the 2020s. Our story starts with the original rock 'n' roll craze, handily helped along by the country's U.S. Army base, before we go to Iceland's own 1960s beat boom (which spawned, among others, the mightily named Thor's Hammer, Iceland's first musical export attempt) and its later turn to folk and prog-influenced performers, who used as sources not only Icelandic folklore and folk songs, but their mother tongue, addressing some very real Icelandic social issues. Like elsewhere, the emergence of punk had seismic effects on Icelandic music, later giving birth to The Sugarcubes and Björk. The latter's international solo career then paved the way for more acts, Sigur Rós being the most obvious example.

The last decade brought us the highest internationally charting Icelandic band of all time, Of Monsters and Men, and the 2020s have been dominated by Laufey, the globetrotting phenomenon who has brought millions of fans into the orbit of post-war jazz while she casually plays cello with Billy Joel and receives a Grammy statue from Rufus Wainwright.

To accurately comprehend the progressive, experimental leanings of Sigur Rós, we must know about Iceland's unique post-punk scene and the country's very own 1970s prog-rock greats, as both of these musical strands inspired 'our golden boys', a fact that's well-known to 'us' but may be less familiar internationally. This account is therefore not just historical, as the surroundings, the social environment, traditions and an indescribable but very real 'Icelandic' spirit infuses the music-making as well. To understand the characteristics of Icelandic popular music, we have to understand the place that it belongs to. Its heritage, language, social construction and the realities of a microsociety, directed by a 'village' factor that both frees musicians up and constricts them, makes for a noticeable lack of bureaucratic formalities in terms of general communication, cultural institutions and so on, underpinning vibrant and active scenes where musicians move freely between genres.[5] The country also has a distinctive place among the Nordic countries, a fringe nation of sorts along with Finland while Norway, Denmark and Sweden are more clustered, market- and culture-wise. A European country, but always quite Americanized as well, as we will see in the chapter about the 1950s.

The opportunity to dispel some of the persistent myths about the Icelandic popular music culture – from laymen and academics alike – is a welcome one. It's not all nature and northern lights, geysers and molten lava, elves and quirky wool-sweater-wearing poets, no matter how desperately people want it to be thus. The image bestowed upon the Icelandic musician (and Icelandic music) has been a source of mortification, laughs and even some monetary opportunities over the years, where the sometimes mythical qualities and 'Borealistic'[6] fascination towards Iceland's popular music scene is a source of conflict, an internal tug of war for the musicians where their identity and creative means can be jumbled up and thrown off course.[7] Even bands like Sigur Rós haven't resisted the urge to poke some fun at this situation, their tour announcements sometimes written with tongues firmly in cheek, promising 'epic, transcendental' nights and so on. This is a gesture that possibly goes over the heads of some fans but is easily decoded by those in the know.

Some play merrily up to the myth, taking the 'let's give them what they want' stance with a knowing wink. It can be quite the savvy business move. After all, if a glacier on the cover helps to sell more copies, why not? Others denounce it, simply tired of being asked to ride a horse on the hillside or pose in a lava field, having been holed up in a Reykjavík cellar most of their teenage years, listening to The Velvet Underground rather than to the sounds of waterfalls. Yes, urban kids are here in droves with a specifically urban outlook on life, where nature and romanticism are a long way away.

I stress that the aim of this book is to explore the history of Icelandic *popular* music and place it within both internal and external contexts. There are other worlds in Icelandic music culture that, for the sake of space and clarity, I will only touch upon if necessary. Jazz and classical, that's another book and not for me to write. I will mention some artists who have bridged worlds: Jóhann Jóhannsson is one of them, but jazz musicians like ADHD and Skúli Sverrisson, experimentalists like Hafdís Bjarnadóttir, composers like Bára Gísladóttir, all of whom have worked within the popular music world to some extent, won't get any in-depth coverage.

This book is informed by my lifelong affiliation with the Icelandic popular music scene from many and varied angles. Most importantly by my 25-year-long career as a music journalist and the experience, knowledge, insights and connections I have accumulated in that time, combined with my more recent work as a socio-musicologist. To be honest, we, the Icelanders, are simply chuffed that people have a real interest in what we are doing up here musically. But now, let's go to the heart of the matter. On we go. *Áfram með smjörið!*[8]

Introduction: Music in Iceland, from the Beginning to the Popular Music Age

What follows is a brief look at music-making in Iceland in a broader historical context, which serves to get a better and even more insightful grasp on the subject at hand. Popular music-making, the Anglo-American pop/rock variety, is the focus of the book but here we will trace Icelandic music history from the absolute beginning up until our first chapter, when rock 'n' roll takes hold.

Scholars have described musical life in Iceland since its settlement in AD 874 in quite some detail.[1] Iceland was Christianized in approximately AD 1000 and with that, church singing was introduced – Gregorian chants in the Roman Catholic tradition. Little is known about the musical traditions of the pagan Vikings that preceded this church singing, although the unique Icelandic form of *tvísöngur* (twin-song or two-part singing) is believed to have been practised at the time.[2] With the Lutheran Reformation in the sixteenth century, Catholic singing was supplanted by an updated Protestant form.

Our knowledge of the Icelandic traditional music or folk music – the 'popular' music of the medieval ages if you will – can be attributed to the pioneering work of one man, the Reverand Bjarni Þorsteinsson, who systematically collected Icelandic folk songs in the late nineteenth century and published them in the years 1906–9, constituting a sprawling 950-page book. Bjarni's drive in this enormous task was derived from the fact that he noticed that his school colleagues had given up on the old Icelandic songs in favour of Scandinavian and German tunes that infiltrated the country in the Romantic period.[3] Icelandic folk songs were heavily influenced by old church modes, taking cues from hymns and psalms, often characterized by a certain heaviness and melancholia.[4] Because of Iceland's cultural isolation in this period, musical forms remained static for centuries; new strands and advancements in music culture taking place in Europe did not reach the country.

One form of folk music was unique to Iceland. The *rímur* (rhymes) first came to prominence in the fourteenth century and proved to be quite popular through the ages. The *rímur* are 'long cycles of poetic verse delivered in a distinctively Icelandic half sung/half chanted style' and are rooted in the country's ancient literature, the epic Sagas and Eddas.[5] The *rímur* method also took on a more streamlined form by addressing everyday subjects such as humorous gossip and raunchy matters and in those instances they were called *rímnalög* (rhyme-songs).[6] The *rímur* were frowned upon by scholars and the literary elite and the form was almost dead and buried come the twentieth century. It survived in closed circles and a society was established in 1929 to preserve it. The society – Iðunn – is still active today and at the very end of the twentieth century the *rímur* form infiltrated the Icelandic pop/rock scene with gusto due to Sigur Rós's interest.[7] On their 2001 spring tour the band featured a *kvæðamaður* or '*rímur* singer' – the chair of Iðunn, Steindór Andersen.[8] A compilation, which saw a teaming up of *rímur* singers and Icelandic rappers, was also released in 2002 (*Rímur & Rapp*).

Instruments were rather scarce in Iceland throughout the centuries, the only constants being small organs used in churches. In homes, the *langspil* (literally meaning 'long-play') was used, a form of drone zither and unique to Iceland (a comparable instrument is the Appalachian dulcimer, also a drone zither).[9] The *langspil* faded from view in the twentieth century but has been revived to a small extent in Icelandic folk music circles. Another similar instrument, unique to Iceland, is a *fiðla* ('fiddle'; confusingly, the same word is used for a violin in Iceland). Very little is known about that instrument, which disappeared, almost completely, in the middle of the nineteenth century.[10]

At the start of the twentieth century Icelanders started to claw their way out of cultural darkness, emerging from their caves, almost literally.[11] Music-wise, changes had begun to take place around the mid-nineteenth century with the emergence of male choirs, which have been an integral part of the Icelandic music culture ever since. Pianos and harmoniums also began to adorn Icelandic homes; Reykjavík – then with a population of a few thousand people – was the centre of all these activities.[12] At the turn of the century, Reykjavík's population was 6,000 but just ten years later the size of the town had doubled. Things began to move swiftly in many aspects of cultural life; students who had been studying in Denmark at the University of Copenhagen – the official capital of Iceland at the time – came home in their droves, bringing with them new ideas and enthusiasm towards the enrichment and internationalization of Iceland's culture.

The period from 1900 to 1930 was marked by steady progression in almost all fields of music. New instruments, schools, people exclusively educated in music, brass bands, choirs, music venues, composers and others; all of this contributed to the modernization of Icelandic music life. Svengalis and larger-than-life characters were often at the forefront of the changes, 'fire-souls' as the Faroese call it (*eldsál*).[13]

At the end of that significant era, Icelanders were starting to enjoy a steady stream of foreign artists, some of great renown, who gave concerts to an ever-growing population of music fans in the capital. In 1925 Hljómsveit Reykjavíkur (the Reykjavík Orchestra) was founded, eventually leading to the Iceland Symphony Orchestra, which was established in 1950, something that the original orchestra leaders had aimed for from the very beginning.[14] Two important markers, both from the year 1930, conclude this period. First, the foundation of the Icelandic National Broadcasting Service, that is, the Icelandic state radio (RÚV), and second, the foundation of the very first music school in Iceland, the Reykjavík Music School. The formation of the school was a solution to a fairly practical problem – people who were to join the Reykjavík Orchestra, formed five years earlier, needed to be taught how to play their instruments.[15] It is also worth mentioning that the pioneering composer Jón Leifs became active in this period. A true fire-soul, he was relentless in his efforts in advancing Icelandic music culture. His temperament was not unlike his epic, unforgiving music, and his life was littered with controversies. Friendships were lost, enemies were gained but he never wavered from the great cause of enriching Icelandic music life. He founded STEF (Composers' Rights Society of Iceland), equivalent to PRS for Music (a copyright collective) in the UK, collected Icelandic folk songs and gave the very first symphonic concerts in Iceland in the summer of 1926. Educated in Leipzig, he started his career as a composer and is best known for his large orchestral works, drawing heavily from Icelandic nature and the sagas.[16]

Around 1930 Reykjavík had begun to mimic international music trends. Cafés provided live music for their guests, with light music during the day and jazz in the evenings. Slowly but surely, the Icelanders themselves started to handle all of these duties, rather than relying on imported professionals. A growing number now sought music education in Europe and introduced their fellow countrymen to what they had been exposed to on the continent. Icelandic choirs were beginning to match their Scandinavian counterparts and Icelandic musicians were getting ever more skilled, even though most of them had to make do with a semi-professional career.[17] The best of them, like the opera singer Pétur Á. Jónsson, made inroads into Germany and sang in opera houses for decades.[18] An early example of an 'escape' from the stifling realities that talents face in small communities.[19]

In the 1930s more music institutions emerged, such as Tónlistarfélagið (The Music Society), an all-encompassing entity established in 1932 by twelve culture enthusiasts and assigned to oversee various music activities like the music school, the Reykjavík Orchestra and so on. This group also founded the Icelandic Musicians Union (FÍH, also in 1932), still very active today, which protects the rights of musicians of every type. Icelandic Music scholar Bjarki Sveinbjörnsson notes:

> The year 1930 is a pinnacle in Icelandic music history, where we see the end of a slow, one-hundred-year development of Icelandic music, bringing it into modern times. Many of the music institutions that characterize other Western societies see the light of day around that time. More would follow in the coming years . . . the development of Icelandic music culture in the twentieth century is a good example of how these things progress in Western societies, but the timespan is much shorter.[20]

1

The 1950s: Rock from the Base

The country was still a relatively young nation when rock 'n' roll emerged, having achieved full independence from Denmark in 1944 after being its colony – and, prior to that, one of Norway's – since the thirteenth century. The independence struggle had begun in earnest in the nineteenth century and Iceland became a sovereign state in 1918. In 1944, when Europe was in the throes of the Second World War and Denmark was occupied by Nazi Germany, the Icelandic parliament Alþingi (Althing) decided to sever all ties with its old rulers. In a referendum, 99.5 per cent were in favour of abolishing the Act of Union.[1] The country had a total population of 120,000 at the time.

Incidentally, Iceland was occupied as well, but by the allies. The British Army seized the country in 1940, to be replaced by the U.S. Army a year later. The USA had a base – a naval air station – in Iceland right up until 2006, just outside of Keflavík, a small town (population *c.* 20,000 in 2024 but in 1940 a mere 1,500) some 40 kilometres (25 mi.) from Reykjavík. Iceland's only international airport is near Keflavík and was built by the U.S. Army in 1943. The impact of the U.S. Army on Iceland, both socially and culturally, was substantial: 'Iceland at the beginning of the war was a poor, backward society. The Americans brought in cars, films, music, Coca Cola – and lots of money. Suddenly there was ample employment and Icelanders became wealthy almost overnight.'[2]

The base had its own radio and television station; the former started broadcasting in 1951 and the latter in 1955 – a full eleven years before Icelandic National Television began operations. Some procedures were made for the signals to reach as little outside of the base as possible but to no avail. The signal was strong in the southwest corner of Iceland, including the capital, but was especially strong in Keflavík, a vehicle in turning the town into Iceland's own 1960s Liverpool, with a strong and vibrant music scene, far exceeding the one in the capital, which lacked a steady signal and thus the steady diet of new pop and rock music. The capital had access to national radio, like the rest of the country, but it shunned the popular music of the day, partly explaining why Reykjavík was struggling to keep up with a small nearby town in terms of cultural modernity. In 1959 selected members of the parliament even made some efforts to try to get the broadcasts banned, and in that year the Icelandic government erected a 3-metre (10 ft) 'quarantine' fence around the Keflavík base to stave off 'cultural pollution'.[3]

But Icelanders, just like many other non-Anglo-American nations in the Western world, embraced these cultural influences. Icelandic versions of Elvis Presley sprang up and – on a practical note – a job was to be had for Icelandic musicians at the base, as the Americans paid better than the Icelanders did.[4] The closeness of and relatively easy access to such forbidden fruits, especially early on, ensured that the base became a breeding ground for cross-cultural musical exchange, particularly benefiting the blue-eyed Icelanders. As it happens, the first time a rock singer reared his head in the country, he was from the motherland or, rather, the base. Dean Bowling, an American soldier on leave from the base, sang a few rock songs, 'Rock Around the Clock' and the like, with one of the more established Icelandic dance bands of the day, Carl Billich's band, in December 1955.[5] Bowling's performances were a relatively swift introduction to the form; Bill Haley's version of 'Rock Around the Clock' was originally released in 1954 (as a B-side) but didn't take off properly until 1955, the same year as Bowling took to the Icelandic stage. We can but speculate how soon rock 'n' roll would have arrived, had the army not been stationed here.

One of Iceland's most prominent and best-loved singers at the time, Haukur Morthens (who would go on to become a proper musical legend), was the first person to play a rock 'n' roll track on the radio when Elvis's 'Heartbreak Hotel' got a spin on his weekly national radio programme in early 1956. Apparently an old farmer in the southeast had a stroke upon hearing it.[6] Icelandic sailors also brought the good stuff from America, and American rock films were shown as early as 1957 (arriving here before they were shipped to

Haukur Morthens was one of Iceland's most beloved singers. This EP was released in 1958 and contains four 'rocking' tracks in Icelandic.

other Scandinavian countries, a fact that underpins the high Americanization of Icelandic culture), and teenagers duly tried to cause a riot, just like their American counterparts.[7] Icelanders also got their first taste of live rock music in 1957 when British jazz musician Tony Crombie brought his newly established rock 'n' roll band The Rockets to the country and played several shows to thousands of rock-crazed teenagers. With the police being called in on several occasions to restore order, Icelanders proved themselves quick to replicate the means and behaviours of like-minded teenagers from around the world, dancing in the theatre aisles, ripping up the seats and generally being unruly.[8] An eagerness to play with 'the big boys' was evident in the Icelanders' overall demeanour. As a fresh-faced nation still learning to find its footing after centuries of foreign rule, they eagerly embraced something new and different with both hands. Like the little brother who is allowed to play with his elder brother and his gang of friends, he is keen to show that 'he can do it too.' This attitude is deeply rooted in the sensibility of Icelanders and usually takes flight at international sporting events, or when a musician succeeds abroad, for example. No wonder that Henry Kissinger referred to Iceland in his memoirs as the most arrogant small nation he had ever encountered.[9]

Established home-grown musicians followed the general consensus of the elders and condemned the musical barbarism that was rock 'n' roll, hoping that the fad would evaporate quickly. But as professionals they were forced to play the style and this they did, albeit grudgingly. No band wholly devoted to rock 'n' roll was established in these years but instead the existing dance bands invited hopeful young singers to sing a song or two with them on stage. Similar developments could be seen and heard in Scandinavia. The first Icelanders to make something of a career as rock singers, if short-lived, were Þorsteinn Eggertsson and Siggi Johnnie. Þorsteinn was duly called 'The Icelandic Elvis'. (Another Icelandic Elvis, Óli 'Presley' Ágústsson, graced the stage at the end of 1956, a little before

Þorsteinn and Siggi, and is the first Icelandic rock singer mentioned in documents.[10]) Þorsteinn would later become the most prolific lyric writer in Icelandic, penning hundreds of lyrics for various bands and singers, churning them out in the 1960s and '70s.

Þorsteinn came from Keflavík and the proximity to the base had made him more fluent in English than his peers in the capital and helped him pick up American idioms. He despised how people mimed the lyrics aimlessly without understanding the words and duly began to write Icelandic lyrics to the songs.[11] Often loosely translated, in many cases going for phonetic aestheticism rather than strict translations (for instance, 'Return to Sender' became 'Þrjú tonn af sandi', meaning 'three tons of sand', a sentence that made for the right number of syllables rather than a poetic emulation of the original). These were the first attempts at using this small Nordic language in a rock setting. Sadly Þorsteinn never got to make his own records.

Similarly, while Siggi Johnnie did not manage to actually record, he was a full-on rocker, making a living out of music and establishing the first all-out rock band, Fimm í fullu fjöri (The Fully Alive Five).[12] The band mostly performed at the base, simply because it paid better. Siggi and the band used to record songs from the radio on tape in a bid to capture the latest hits, and he then learnt the words like a parrot, imitating sounds rather than singing lyrics. 'Our American audience didn't seem to mind that I was basically just sputtering nonsense.'[13]

Eventually, a bona fide Icelandic rock song was recorded, but it had little to do with the fury that was imbued in the young rockers mentioned above. Instead, an established Icelandic pop singer, Erla Þorsteinsdóttir, was marched into a studio in 1957 to record the song 'Vagg og velta', a direct Icelandic translation of the words 'rock and roll'. The song was a version of Bill Haley's spin on 'When the Saints Go Marching In', 'The Saints Rock 'n' Roll'. The song was promptly banned, not due to its aural assault but because of its lyrics, which

Singer Siggi Johnnie was a leading figure in the Icelandic rock 'n' roll scene, known for his powerful voice and undeniable swagger.

Erla Þorsteins (Erla Þorsteinsdóttir) was the first Icelander to sing a bona fide rock 'n' roll song when 'Vagg og velta' was released in 1957.

featured lines from some of Iceland's most beloved poets. The ban naturally made the single sell by the truck-load.[14]

The first Icelandic singer to release records that truly embodied rock 'n' roll – with the right attitude, singing style and flair – was Skapti Ólafsson, who cut six sides in 1957 and 1958 (as Skafti Ólafsson).[15] One of the tracks, 'Allt á floti' ('Everything's Soaked'), a version of Tommy Steele's 'Water, Water', was banned as well because of the hidden (or not-so-hidden) sexual innuendo. Despite this, the song became very popular, a radio staple in Iceland to this day. Skafti's records were released by Iceland's first record label, Íslenzkir tónar (Icelandic Tones), which was in business from 1947 to 1965, releasing a variety of records; pop, rock, jazz and classical, all of which featured the most prominent artists of the day.

A little after Skafti Ólafsson's triumphs, there was a shift in the dance market – rock 'n' roll bands became prevalent, made up of young musicians who had an emotional affinity to rock 'n' roll as a respectable musical outlet. Lúdó og Stefán (Lúdó and Stefán) were a good example of this and came to prominence at the tail end of the decade. Ragnar Bjarnason (Raggi Bjarna) also began his musical career this decade and would become one of Iceland's best-loved singers, a national treasure capable of crooner-like ballads, rock 'n' roll and everything in between. His disarming, joyous style made it possible for him to embrace modernity when it came knocking and he joined rappers and rockers who could be his grandchildren on stage without hesitation.

The 1950s was a decade that saw rapid changes in Icelandic society. The country enjoyed an unprecedented economic boom aided by, among other things, the Marshall Plan, the American initiative to rebuild Western Europe after the Second World War. Reykjavík had around 50,000 inhabitants at the time and aerial photos of 'the city' show freshly erected apartment buildings throughout. In between are operational farmsteads, looking like trespassers, and decaying, deserted army camps, used into the 1970s by Reykjavík's poor.[16] This shame-bound part of Reykjavík's history has been a constant inspiration for popular songs, films and books.

Icelanders were quick to adapt to cultural fashions from abroad, a need that seemed particularly intense immediately after gaining independence. The new-found sense of freedom gave way to various efforts to distance the fast-changing Icelandic society from Danish influences and home-grown institutions were established to meet that aim. There came a renewed sense of Icelandic self, even if it meant replicating foreign strands quite closely. Record labels and affiliated stores exemplified this shift; prior to that, records by Icelandic singers had been released by Danish and British labels.

Popular music programmes were debuted on national radio and, at the start of the decade, song competitions were established, giving boost to popular music songwriting. In the year 1950, the Iceland Symphony Orchestra played its first concert and the National Theatre was opened. Two years prior, STEF, the Composers' Rights Society of Iceland, was established.

Rock 'n' roll continued to seep into the Icelandic psyche in the coming years, as was the case around the world. Come the 1960s, another cultural revolution was just around the corner, but this time stemming from the other side of the pond, namely Liverpool.

2

The 1960s: We Got the Beat (as Well)

In the 1960s Icelanders continued to emulate Anglo-American popular music. Every self-respecting Western society had their 'Beatles' and the Icelandic ones came from Keflavík, nicknamed 'the Liverpool of Iceland' in music circles because of its unusually high activity on the pop and rock front compared to the capital. This made the town the hotbed for an exciting, all Icelandic, trimmed-down beat boom (and making it, rather than the capital, the hometown of The Icelandic Museum of Rock 'n' Roll, which opened in 2014).

Keflavík was a small, nondescript town before the upheavals of the Second World War. Lava blankets most of the Reykjanes peninsula, where Keflavík lies, and the town and surrounding villages have relied almost exclusively on the fishing industry throughout the centuries. Volcanic activity has always been high in the area and at the time of writing one of the bigger municipalities, Grindavík, has become uninhabitable because of constant eruptions.

The massive U.S. Army operations at the time, literally across the road from Keflavík, shook these grey fishing towns to their core, not just economically but culturally. They quickly became highly dependent on the jobs created by the army, and to this day the airport remains a substantial provider in that respect. People 'experienced a completely different food culture, made American friends, and smuggled American duty-free goods from the base'.[1] To highlight the impact all of this had on young, aspiring musicians in the town, the aforementioned museum features a map showing how many of the most influential Icelandic musicians lived in close proximity, usually one or two blocks from each other.

After a brief twilight of sharply dressed, well-behaved and synchronized Shadows-inspired bands, the primal and revolutionary energy of The Beatles took hold here as elsewhere. Iceland's Beatles were called Hljómar (The Chords) and were formed in 1963 by one Gunnar Þórðarson (then seventeen years old) after leaving his 'Shadows' band (aptly named Skuggar, which literally means shadows in Icelandic). Staying true to the raw, amateur spirit of the early beat groups, he hired his best friend as the bass player, considering the fact that this friend had never seen a bass guitar before to be only a minor concern. The bass player, Rúnar Júlíusson, was to become one of the most legendary figures in Icelandic rock, deeply loved by generations old and new. Hljómar quickly rehearsed a set of Beatles covers, which they duly played four nights in a row in a Reykjavík cinema in March 1964, alongside other up-and-coming bands, while those in attendance, mostly teenagers, did their best to mimic the Beatles craze. The rest of 1964 was theirs for the taking, and the band played so frequently that the young members were able to make a living from it.[2] Gunnar wrote most of the songs himself, taking a cue from The Beatles, and the lyrics, initially, were in Icelandic.

The band's first single was released in February 1965 by the recently established label SG-hljómplötur (SG-Records), which had been founded in 1964 and was kind of a successor to Íslenzkir tónar, which folded in 1965. The label name contains the initials of Svavar Gestsson – Iceland's foremost music mogul and entrepreneur in the 1960s and '70s. As a band leader, record company executive and all-round Svengali, Svavar did a lot for Icelandic pop music when it was taking its first steps and his label was more or less the only one in the country that actively released such music in that era. The single was a landmark release, as it featured two original compositions by

Gunnar, an all-out beat rocker, 'Fyrsti kossinn' ('The First Kiss'), and a tender ballad, 'Bláu augun þín' ('Your Blue Eyes'). Both songs are considered classics in the Icelandic popular music canon. The year 1965 was Iceland's 1964 in a sense: the year the country became flooded with Beatles-type bands – a year later than the blitz that hit the UK. The arrival of international music fads to Iceland has been a belated one in most cases, a buffer of one or two years, sometimes longer (five years in the case of punk, much longer in the case of hip-hop). But sometimes, music genres have grown and thrived simultaneously with their evolution in other countries.

Popular music as a driving cultural force was evolving at a rapid pace in the 1960s. Teenagers, as a powerful social entity, were coming to the forefront, both here and elsewhere. Icelandic society was quite sensitive to external influences in the first decades after

Hljómar, the Icelandic Beatles, in full regalia.

the war and the importance of foreign musical visits in these innocent times cannot be overestimated. The effects could be seismic, a single gig a revolutionary one, inspiring local musicians to take up instruments and follow a similar path. The 1960s was in no way different from the 1950s in these matters. The most noteworthy visit was by The Kinks in September 1965, the band at the top of its game. The band played in Austurbæjarbíó (the East-Side Cinema), an important live venue for decades to come. Other bands paid a visit, mostly second-tier groups like The Swinging Blue Jeans, The Searchers and The Tremeloes. Herman's Hermits and The Hollies played as well and films like The Beatles' *A Hard Day's Night* also played a substantial part in schooling the emerging Icelandic hipster, just like the rock 'n' roll films had done ten years before.

Hljómar's reign over the Icelandic beat era was total; other bands followed but Hljómar led the way, both artistically and in terms of popularity. By the summer of 1965 the group had effectively exhausted all avenues, having been at it relentlessly for a year and a half. Naturally, the number of venues available for artists to perform at in a Scandinavian backwoods society is limited. Iceland's size means that it doesn't take long for a band to play all the main venues twice, to effectively the same crowd. In need of new challenges and new audiences, Hljómar naturally looked abroad, like talented Icelandic musicians have done before and since. Renaming themselves Thor's Hammer, they auditioned for Parlophone – appropriately enough, The Beatles' label in Britain – and promptly secured a record deal. An American manager (from the base, where else?) brokered the deal. The label released a couple of 7-inch singles in 1966 (and Columbia released one in the USA in 1967) but all of them sank without a trace. The music is simply wonderful, brashly played freakbeat nuggets making it apparent that Gunnar and the band were absolutely keeping up with the times. The guitar is drenched in fuzzbox effects, coming on like a buzz-saw, and one song ends in a feedback frenzy: true proto-punk mayhem. This sonic sojourn was a one-off; Hljómar focused on more mainstream music when they returned to Iceland and these 7-inch singles are sought-after collector's items today.[3]

These export activities also produced a surreal short film, *Umbarumbamba*, which was themed around the *sveitaball* gathering, or country dance, a phenomenon deeply entrenched in the rural areas of Iceland where a band plays the popular hits of the day to drunken locals in the community's gathering hall.[4] These dances were a significant part of the livelihood of Iceland's most popular bands over the decades, especially during the summer season. However, they have diminished in popularity over the last twenty years. The film made no impact and was quickly forgotten.

Such efforts by Hljómar have of course been replicated to some extent by later musicians, and as can be seen, an awareness of the selling points of Icelandic heritage was already in place, as the band name 'Thor's Hammer' proves. The adventure, in many ways ill-advised but at least producing enduring music in those psych nuggets, cost them their popularity in the home market. With Hljómar defunct, other bands quickly moved in. Keflavík was still the stronghold in terms of productivity and prominence and the kids from the capital found themselves travelling to Keflavík on a regular basis, attending gigs.[5] Reykjavík finally had its say, however, as a homegrown group was the next big thing. Dátar (Soldiers) filled the gap left by Hljómar with grace, releasing two EPs in 1966 and 1967, each filled with terrific songs, all in Icelandic bar one.[6] The band was led by a teenage prodigy, Rúnar Gunnarsson, who was just around eighteen when he wrote the material, most of which continues to hold an evergreen status. It is brilliantly melodic songwriting with an originality that escaped mere beat-boom copycatting. Another noteworthy group is Flowers, formed in 1967. Although the band didn't release an album during their two-year lifespan (one EP in 1968), they gained quite a lot of popularity, rivalling Hljómar. Ultimately, this led to a supergroup merger between the two bands at the end of the decade (Trúbrot).[7]

DÁTAR!

Karl - Stefán - Rúnar - Jón Pétur

Dátar klæðast fötum frá Herrahúsinu Aðalstræti 4

DANSLEIKUR

DÁTAR LEIKA MÚSIK VIÐ ALLRA HÆFI!

Dátar was the only beat group that could match the mighty Hljómar in popularity. This poster from 1966 advertises a gig where Dátar are said to play 'music that anyone can enjoy!'

Hljómar returned in 1967, eager to capture their former status, and in this they succeeded. The music was deliberately streamlined this time around; fuzz and freakbeat were out and a more commercially viable route was taken (the band even emphasized covers rather than their fine originals at the inevitable country dances). The return was sealed with a special performance for Icelandic National Television and the band was eager to showcase that they were keeping up with the latest trends. Flowerpots hung from the guitars, the members moustached and wearing flashy hippy clothes. The audience nodded along in unison, the act a clear reference to the famed television appearance by The Beatles performing 'All You Need Is Love' in the summer.[8] That November, Hljómar were the first Icelandic beat group to release an LP, the resulting eponymous affair Iceland's 'first modern pop album'.[9] Ambitions were high and the band was flown to London to record at Chappell Recording Studios, as the only real studio in Iceland at the time was the one at the national radio station. The resultant music aligned with Hljómar's audience-friendly approach, a mix of up-tempo rockers and ballads, and seven out of twelve tracks were covers with Icelandic lyrics (ranging from 'California Dreamin'' to 'Nowhere Man', and 'Call Me', made famous by Petula Clark). There was no Icelandic album released in 1967 or even later to match the adventurousness of *Sgt. Pepper's Lonely Hearts Club Band* or similar albums; only small strands of it were embraced by the Icelanders. The album cover was the closest thing to the psychedelic style popular in the UK at the time, the design a mix of *Revolver* and *Sgt. Pepper*.

Hljómar were not done with their export efforts and in 1968 they made a trip to Sweden that was even more surreal than their doomed short film (where bassist Rúnar Júlíusson had donned a full Viking outfit). This time around the band joined forces with fashion mogul Guðlaugur Bergmann, who was running the clothing store Karnabær (a twist on London's fashion Mecca, Carnaby Street). The following was stated in a news item in the Icelandic daily newspaper *Morgunblaðið*: 'Hljómar will all be dressed in sheepskin-vests. Knitted sock-shoes, caps, etc. will be brought along. Hljómar have arranged for ancient Icelandic rhyme motifs to be added to their music and the langspil [the ancient Icelandic instrument] will be taken along.'[10] Needless to say, nothing substantial came out of the trip, but once again Hljómar managed to predict some of the strands that would shape Icelandic popular music-making in the future.

While responding to the beat boom in the UK, Icelanders simultaneously took note of the folk revival in the USA and Savanna tríóið (Savanna Trio) were effectively a home-grown version of the Kingston Trio; the Icelandic threesome started out in 1963, just like Hljómar. The members were the same age as Hljómar's members, the band formed in high school and became an overnight sensation, changing mop tops and scruffiness for neatly pressed suits and silky harmonies. The trio became very popular in the latter half of the 1960s and were inclined to put an Icelandic stamp on their material. To this end, their first record – the second LP to be released by SG-hljómplötur – was called *Folksongs from Iceland* and contained arrangements of well-known Icelandic folk songs, many of them taken from the fabled collection of the Rev. Bjarni Þorsteinsson (we'll look closer at Bjarni's salvation work in the next chapter and how Icelandic popular musicians made use of it). This approach of theirs would echo, if indirectly, down the decades, particularly when Icelandic musicians began to flaunt their heritage, rather than conceal it by mimicking the Anglo-American popular music fads of the day. The group wrote their own songs, using old poems as lyrics, and would also delve into folk music from other countries. The Savanna tríóið debut was the finest – and in reality, the only – introduction to Icelandic folk music so far, frowned upon by the purist elite of course.[11] Its success lies in its nonchalant and honest approach, a genuine attempt at presenting this music to foreigners, as mentioned in the liner notes by Svavar Gestsson, the label's owner:

> As few Icelandic singers have appeared overseas and the recording of Icelandic music has still left many fields more or less untouched many of the peculiar Icelandic folk-songs have never been heard outside Iceland. Many visitors to Iceland in recent years have been enchanted by this outstanding heritage, not least when they have heard it interpreted by the Savanna Trio . . . It became evident at the very first concert that in the Savanna Trio Iceland had acquired a group that was in no way inferior to overseas groups of similar nature.[12]

The group was hugely successful in Iceland. They even made a trip to the UK and performed at the BBC in 1965, playing for 22 million on the show *Tonight*, hosted by their fellow countryman, Magnús Magnússon.[13]

The beat boom and the folk boom ran parallel to each other, Hljómar and Savanna tríóið occasionally sharing a stage.[14] The groups were on friendly terms and Þórir Baldursson, one of the Savanna members, also from Keflavík, was Rúnar Júlíusson's brother-in-law. He would go on to have quite a remarkable career, particularly in the 1970s.[15] This connection is a succinct symbol of the close-knit nature of Iceland's music culture, where the small but different worlds lie in close proximity and can rub off on each other, family-, friendship- and creativity-wise.

It's therefore intriguing to note the lack of crossover of folk and rock bands during this decade. While this path was laid by Bob Dylan, The Byrds and others in the United States, in Iceland the pop/rock and folk scenes remained separate music-wise. When the Savannas disbanded in 1967, they were succeeded by another trio, Ríó tríó, from Kópavogur, a town just south of Reykjavík. Ríó tríó brought a more upbeat vibe and their lyrics often had a playful, humorous tone. Ríó (as it was sometimes abbreviated to) would fast become the people's band, securing that position well into the 1970s. Protest songs were curiously absent in the latter half of the

1960s as well.[16] One woman, Kristín A. Ólafsdóttir, known as the Icelandic Joan Baez, released an EP in 1968 in that style and a young actor, Hörður Torfason, would become very active in that field at the start of the 1970s.

Trúbrot was a true supergroup and engaged tastefully with current musical trends. This photo is from the back cover of their debut album of the same name (1969).

3

The 1970s: Folkloric Prog and Socio-Realistic Pop

The year 1969 proved to be a pivotal one in Icelandic pop and rock music. The 1960s ended in a seismic way, much like in other Western countries, with the obligatory student protests and a gradually widening generational gap. At the end of the year, a symbolic musical shift took place. The energetic innocence of the beat groups and the carefree psychedelia that followed had been slowly giving way to heavier leanings and a more thoughtful stance. Five days before Christmas an album arrived in stores that proved to be a watershed. Trúbrot's (Breach of Faith) eponymous debut album contains an amalgam of styles, chamber pop with compulsory flutes, stomping proto-hard rock, jazz flourishes and the odd cover version (The Beatles, The Supremes, José Feliciano). The arrangements are quite varied and progressive, complex leanings battle for attention with straightforward hit material.

To reinforce the notion that the band were serious, a version of 'The Pilgrim's Chorus' found in Richard Wagner's opera *Tännhauser* was included on the album, which closed with an obligatory ten-minute freak-out. The album cover is enchanting, presented in a gatefold sleeve, which was a novelty in Iceland at the time. An arty, cream-coloured front cover contains photos of the members and a disparate collection of white painted things like a doll, Coca-Cola bottles and some apples. All the songs' lyrics are in Icelandic and the mixture of styles served like a bridge between the closing decade and the one that was around the corner.

Trúbrot was a supergroup, made up of members from two of the most prominent groups in the 1960s – Hljómar and Flowers – and they led the 'serious' rock charge at the beginning of the 1970s. The old childhood friends from Hljómar, songwriter and guitarist Gunnar Þórðarson and bassist/singer and all-round 'rocker' Rúnar Júlíusson, had made a pact with two Flowers members, organ and drum prodigies Karl Sighvatsson and Gunnar Jökull Hákonarson, to join them in an original and challenging band. The icing on this bona fide hippy/prog-rock cake was singer Shady Owens, who had joined Hljómar years earlier. Shady was half Icelandic, half American (the daughter of an American soldier) so the English pronunciation in the singing was flawless and the Icelandic singing even more bewitching, as Sandy's accent gave it an exotic vibe. Gunnar Jökull had drummed with The Syn (a pre-Yes band) in the 1960s and contributed to their singles but declined to join the ranks of Yes, a story that's often repeated in Icelandic pop-lore. Trúbrot was *the* band and its musicians were the only Icelanders of their ilk that had any foreign experience to speak of. Putting the connections that Hljómar had made in previous years to good use, the album was recorded in the recently opened Trident Studios in London. Tony Visconti, who later produced David Bowie, arranged the brass and the strings, and the album was recorded in an unbelievable fifteen hours.

During this period, Iceland welcomed several renowned musical guests from abroad, who were typically greeted with great enthusiasm. This was accentuated by a sort of gratitude towards the musicians for simply acknowledging the existence of the country and gracing it with their presence – a stance which is surprisingly dominant to this day. These visits proved positive, if only to infuse the locals with new ideas and eagerness to create something by themselves (think the initial visit of punk pioneers the Sex Pistols to Manchester for instance, where every other punter formed a band in its wake). In 1970 Led Zeppelin played at the Reykjavík Arts Festival, shortly before they became the fully-fledged rock gods we know. The concert would prove to be a major event, egging on home-grown Zeppelin-inspired acts. 'Immigrant Song', the opening track on *Led Zeppelin III* (1970), details that very visit with mentions of the land of ice and snow, hot springs, midnight sun and so on. The song immediately entered the annals of Icelandic popular music history and for a nation that's barely detectable on maps or population registries, 'recognitions' like this are always held very dear and frequently revisited when Icelanders need to nurture their collective national psyche. Other significant bands that visited Iceland in the early 1970s include Procol Harum, Slade, Deep Purple and Badfinger.

Trúbrot, just like Hljómar before them, had set the scene and more bands followed. Long-haired, bearded men (yes, mostly men of course) started to make an appearance in Iceland's music scene, their stern faces and 'thinking man's' poses evident in photographs. Song titles like 'Dark Roses' and band names like Náttúra (Nature) and Tilvera (Existence) were all the rage. Trúbrot were to meet some worthy challengers as the greatest rock group in Iceland at the start of the 1970s and one of the earliest of these was Óðmenn (Ode-men), who, like most of the members of Trúbrot, traced their origins to Keflavík. At this time, LP releases were quite rare in the pop and rock field but Óðmenn, out of the blue, released a double-sided effort in 1970. The eponymous album contained fifteen songs, the music was proggy rock (not a full-blown prog-rock affair), leaning towards hard-riffing boogie territory, and the musicianship was airtight. The group had roots in the beat boom, going back as far as 1966, but now, as a trio, modelled itself after Cream. The lyrics, all in Icelandic (bar one song), carried with them some acute, if wide-eyed, social commentary, touching on the political topics of the time like war, pollution and third-world poverty. The album is revered to this day as one of the greatest achievements of that era; the record is a cult item, as original vinyl pressings are sparse. It's a popular 'want' in the thriving 1970s Scandinavian progressive rock collector market, as are some other similar Icelandic LPs.

Another worthy contender was Náttúra, Iceland's 'deepest' hippy rock group. Interestingly, Iceland never produced a real prog-rock group in the mould of ELP, Genesis or Yes.[1] Although prog leanings were sometimes to the fore, traces of bluesy rock and acoustic, poppy whimsy were always part of the stew as well.[2] Náttúra released their only album, *Magic Key*, in 1972, a pitch-perfect work absolutely of its time, orbiting the astral plane with dreamlike ease. The band featured among others former Trúbrot members Shady Owens and Karl Sighvatsson, and virtuoso guitarist Björgvin Gíslason who would become a frequent sight in many 1970s bands. Both Trúbrot and Náttúra swapped members (the small Icelandic progressive rock scene was at the mercy of a revolving door policy). In 1971 Trúbrot had released their magnum opus, the concept album *Lifun*, which follows the life cycle of a man from birth to death (what else?).[3] The undertaking was an ambitious one and the band triumphed in all areas. The album was rightly upheld for many years as the greatest achievement in Icelandic pop and rock music, gaining similar status domestically to The Beatles' *Sgt. Pepper*.[4]

Parallel to these 'inward-looking' groups were more hard-rocking ones, like Icecross and Svanfríður, each managing to make an album. Interestingly, although these two albums are pillars in the story of early '70s Icelandic rock, critically acclaimed and having sold respectably at the time, both of them are still to have an official re-release in their home country. Specialist labels abroad, sometimes semi-legal, have provided the international market with releases, proving that no one is a prophet in his own land. Svanfríður's singer, Pétur Kristjánsson, was the son of Kristján Kristjánsson (KK), who was one of the two foremost bandleaders of the 1950s.[5] Pétur was to become one of Iceland's best-loved rock singers and he transcended generations, a charismatic man loved by all; a 24/7 party animal and an all-round good and generous guy rolled into one. Pétur died prematurely in 2004 and The Troggs's 'Wild Thing', his signature song, was played at the funeral. Pétur was a jack of all trades at the end of the 1960s, singing with beat combos, prog groups and hard rockers, and when Svanfríður folded in 1973 he formed Pelican, which was to become Iceland's most popular group, playing relatively lightweight material compared to Svanfríður. The accessibility of the music secured ample radio time and monstrous record sales and Pelican's debut sold 11,000 copies, the highest album sale in Iceland's history until that time.[6] In the mid-1970s Pelican was Iceland's most popular band, cruising around the country and playing country dances. The band even toured the East Coast of the USA, getting in Pétur's own words 'a glimpse of the glory'.[7] But as was wont, a mere glimpse it was. In the 1960s and '70s, the Icelandic media usually wrote intently about the briefest of musical forays onto foreign territories, often with unfounded, speculative tones about inevitable world domination. This naivety would gradually wear off but occasional relapses do surface. Pelican would later morph into the band Paradís (Paradise) and then into Poker (Pétur was quite adamant that the band names should carry his initial). The last incarnation was formed with the sole aim of breaking through overseas, but it was to no avail. In 1977 members of Poker backed a young, unknown singer, called Björk, on her debut album. The singer was only eleven years old, and the album was released locally by the Fálkinn label. In this instance, a world domination of sorts would follow years later. Original copies of this eponymous album are scarce today and change hands for quite an amount.

Pelican were one of the many groups in the 1970s that didn't necessarily aim for heightening of the spirit and deepening of the soul. Icelandic musicians on serious journeys are the ones who have typically enjoyed some coverage from interested foreign music scholars but, like everywhere else, Iceland had its fair share of fun-loving, happy-go-lucky artists that constituted the bulk of the decade's radio fodder, providing the common man's soundtrack to the 1970s.[8]

The mission statement was straightforward: to have good old fun. Some brave souls needed to focus on this essential aspect of pop and rock that's often overlooked when ambition takes over. Ðe lónlí blú bojs (The Lonely Blue Boys) were masters at this game. It says a lot about the realities of the small Icelandic music scene that the group was made up of members from the serious groups mentioned previously, namely Gunnar Þórðarson and Rúnar Júlíusson (them again) from Hljómar/Trúbrot. Engilbert Jensen from Hljómar joined the ranks as well, as did singer Björgvin Halldórsson. Björgvin had been Iceland's most popular singer at the twilight of the 1970s (Björgvin, Bo as he's sometimes called, was to become an ever-constant presence in Icelandic pop in the following years. From around 2000, he emerged as a figure of rock royalty, infusing the essence of Presley and Sinatra with a touch of Johnny Cash's rugged charm). Tired of being skint from making challenging music for unreceptive audiences, the order of the day was fun, pure fun, and to underline this, their debut album, released in 1975, was named after The Beach Boys hit 'Fun, Fun, Fun', translated as 'Stuð Stuð Stuð', an ill-translatable but frequently heard word used to describe something jovial or someone being upbeat and up for it.[9] By replacing artistic ambitions with a bid for a meal ticket, a gargantuan success followed swiftly and many of these songs are radio staples to this day. More bands followed a similar trajectory throughout the 1970s, many of them helmed by former 1960s upstarts who had by now settled into comfy, audience-pleasing roles, much like their colleagues from the USA and the UK. This, as in other parts of the Western pop and rock world, fuelled the flames of the punk revolution that arrived (very belatedly) on these shores.

Gunnar Þórðarson masterminded many projects of this type in the 1970s. A soft pop supergroup (Lummurnar (The Pancakes)), a disco duet (Þú og ég (You and Me)) and some solo albums (which were, admittedly, somewhat more ambitious). Together with Björgvin Halldórsson and Tómas Tómasson (one of the most prominent producers of the 1970s and '80s, and a member of Stuðmenn and Þursaflokkurinn, more of which later) he made two children's records that contained old Icelandic poems set to pop music (as can be seen, the Icelandic folk music heritage was never far from the minds of the popular musicians). These records sold phenomenally well and ended up in every other household. His former partner in crime, Rúnar Júlíusson, also led a good-time band not dissimilar to Ðe lónlí blú bojs called Geimsteinn (Spacestone).[10] It also doubled up as the name of his label, the longest-standing record label in Icelandic history. Finally, Brunaliðið (The Fire Brigade) must be mentioned, a supergroup of sorts that set out to corner the country dance market in 1978. The group was led by Magnús Kjartansson and the order of the day was unapologetic people's music.[11] An album was released in 1978, and it was a smash hit, containing the classic 'Ég er á leiðinni' ('I'm On My Way'), a sailor's melancholic cry for understanding that resonated with the fishing nation. The band experienced a rapid rise to fame but exited the limelight just as quickly. By 1980, after an impressive string of hits, albums and countless country dances, they had folded.

Björgvin sealed his status as one of Iceland's all-time great pop singers in the latter half of the 1970s by releasing records under various guises. Among them was his band Brimkló (literally, 'Surf-Claw'), which went on to become hugely popular. The music was radio-ready and hooky, well-played and exquisitely sung by the charismatic Björgvin and, because of the professionalism involved and the stigma surrounding popular music-making just before the advent of punk, considered the true enemy of worthwhile music-making for decades to come by the critical cognoscenti. It was not until much later that this view shifted somewhat, and for various reasons. Hipsters started to discover new worth in old 1970s Icelandic pop and those who had heaped scorn on Brimkló and their contemporaries' output were by this time mellowing and now looked kindly upon the music, aided by the all-prevailing powers of nostalgia. The alt-country scene of the 2000s also put Brimkló's covers of tunes by Gram Parsons and Merle Haggard into new perspective. Björgvin, tactically, made use of this attitude change and released a fine Brimkló album in 2005, a countrified solo album and two authentic country albums with his band Hjartagosarnir (The Jacks of Hearts) as well.[12]

But Björgvin, like so many of his colleagues, also had his eyes on the prize. Magnús and Jóhann (an Icelandic Simon and Garfunkel of sorts) had been toiling around as Change, releasing exceptionally catchy pop singles in the UK without success. After releasing an LP late in 1974, a deal was snagged from EMI. The band, fully fleshed with our Björgvin and the aforementioned Tómas Tómasson in tow, among other stalwarts from the 1960s, made concerted efforts to break the UK. The now glam-inspired band sported tailor-made, silvery suits in the mould of the Bay City Rollers and Sweet. According to the Icelandic media the band was on the threshold of making it big at the start of 1975 but pre-Internet times involved a lot of guesswork. Icelanders nonetheless watched keenly on the sidelines, like they've done before and since, eagerly hoping that their countrymen would do well in the world. The band returned to Iceland to play the country dances in the summer and was set to return for some promotional efforts in the UK in the autumn. A fairly optimistic yet grounded Magnús described these plans in an interview with an Icelandic daily in August of that year.[13] Upon arriving again in the UK, all of those things quickly fell through. Magnús and Jóhann have worked together to this day and their tender, deeply felt songs continue to resonate with Icelanders.

Iceland in 1975 and the pop/rock landscape was thus: a lot of working bands at home, playing the country dances and releasing generic albums to accompany those activities. Experiments were out, gleeful fun was in. This was the year where most pop/rock scenes in the world were treading water and Iceland was no exception. Fruitless efforts at 'making it' had knocked the wind out of many musicians who were now either licking their wounds or plotting a new strategy.[14] But Iceland – like any other country – also has a healthy dose of bands and artists that don't dream of fame and fortune and are content on their home turf. A good example of this 'non-exportable music' came to the fore in the 1970s. A group that was to become one of Iceland's best-loved bands, an entity that fits neither the ambitious category nor the 'fun fun fun' one, released its debut album in 1976.[15] Mannakorn (referring to manna from heaven) offered just plain good music, pop/rock with the odd blues thrown in.[16] The music wasn't deeply serious, but it also wasn't just carefree fun. Its strength lay first and foremost in the gifted songwriting of Magnús Eiríksson, who has proven to be one of Iceland's most durable songwriters; his unique, idiosyncratic and highly melodic writing, often with a wash of melancholia, struck a chord with every Icelander, no matter what their genre preferences might be. Icelanders will hum unconsciously along to the tunes when hearing them on the radio and the songs are a part of the Icelandic upbringing, so to speak, along with Lýsi cod liver oil and our pure drinking water. The lyrics were and are in Icelandic, often describing everyday vignettes, and they contribute to a certain 'Icelandicness', conveying something that cannot be fully appreciated unless you are deeply rooted in the country's culture. The band, consisting of core members Magnús Eiríksson and singer/bassist Pálmi Gunnarsson, is still going and it's a real shame that the master songcraft of main songwriter, Magnús Eiríksson, will never travel properly.

The same can be applied to singer Vilhjálmur Vilhjálmsson, a certified national treasure. His clear, expressive and – it has to be said – beautiful voice is held in high regard among generations old and new. Vilhjálmur had sung and played with dance hall bands in the 1960s and '70s and had released solo albums as well as albums of duets with his sister Elly. By the mid-1970s he had abandoned singing for a career as an airline pilot, but having guested on said Mannakorn album, his interest in music and performing was

Mannakorn, who have a unique standing in Icelandic popular music, performing live in 1979. Songwriter/guitarist Magnús Eiríksson is to the left, singer/bassist Pálmi Gunnarsson front and centre.

reinvigorated. He began recording again and started to write his own lyrics. His artistry reached its peak on his swansong album, *Hana-nú* (an expression that means something like 'What!?'), released in 1977. Vilhjálmur was killed in a car crash a year later, at 32 years of age, and has been granted legendary status since. His songs are regularly played on the radio, he's the subject of various anniversary and tribute concerts and *Hana-nú* was chosen as the twelfth greatest Icelandic album of all time.[17]

Mannakorn's debut was recorded in a newly opened studio, Hljóðriti (Sound Recorder), which is stationed in Hafnarfjörður, a small town outside of Reykjavík. Hafnarfjörður would become a fertile music town in the years to come, earning a 'rock town' label, and its renowned studio is still in full operation today. For the first time, Icelandic pop musicians had access to a purpose-built recording studio in their own country and didn't have to go abroad to record albums to a professional standard. This would prove to be quite a landmark, as noted by journalist and pop historian Dr. Gunni: 'The opening of the studio was considered a major event at the time . . .

and was by all accounts a big boost for Icelandic music.' Indeed, it was a historical 'build it and they will come' event.[18] This was the only studio of its kind in the 1970s, while there was only one legendary venue/hangout place (Glaumbær or 'Fun Town', which burned down in 1971) and one radio station. Iceland's size makes it impossible to have a rich variety in cultural scenes, a characteristic that is still a constant, even if things have been enriched somewhat in recent times. A culture of 'one' prevails: one major label, one thrash metal band, one Viking metal band and so on.

At the beginning of the decade, a group dubbed Stuðmenn (The Jovial Guys) was put together by two friends as a one-off joke for an upcoming entertainment night at their college, Menntaskólinn við Hamrahlíð. This Reykjavík college is long known for being the 'artiest' of these institutions, breeding many of Iceland's edgiest bands and musicians. A conglomerate of musicians would soon form around the band, also spawning folk-pop band Spilverk þjóðanna (Plaything of the Nations), 'true Icelandic wool sweater music', often abbreviated as Spilverkið, and later folk-rockers Hinn íslenzki þursaflokkur (The Icelandic Troll-Party), usually referred to as Þursaflokkurinn or Þursar/Þursarnir in daily communication.[19] The arrival of these three groups, in 1970, 1974 and 1978 respectively, introduced for the first time an 'Icelandic' identity woven into the music, lyrics and how the members generally acted, talked and carried themselves, gradually building quite the unique artistic stance. A radical idea began to take shape, that worthy pieces of art could be made within the confines of Icelandic reality, inspired by its culture and surroundings, both musically and lyrically. Stuðmenn used a distinctive brand of surreal Icelandic humour in their art, Spilverk þjóðanna – who took a huge artistic leap when they started to sing in Icelandic – would progress to sharp social commentators and Þursaflokkurinn would use old Icelandic folk songs from the well-thumbed collection of the Rev. Bjarni Þorsteinsson, infusing them with the progressive rock of the times.

This turning of the tide was in part because of all the fruitless, exhaustive attempts at breaking ground outside of Iceland, experienced by the members of said bands, both personally and as observers. Modelling yourself after foreign superstars wasn't necessarily the way forward it seemed, and they had now arrived at the conclusion that it was better to spend creative energy at home rather than wasting it on deaf ears abroad. There were indeed some artistic opportunities to be had by concentrating on the home-market.[20] Spilverk þjóðanna had released two fairly generic albums, sung in English, but when they switched to their mother tongue their music grew more popular and simply became better. By surrendering the dream of making it overseas and the compromises that come with it, the members broke free of constraints and a wholly unique (and very Icelandic) musical template was born. Listening to the output established by these individuals over a period of a few years is an astounding experience. The sheer musicality, joy and vibrancy piled on to album after album is remarkable. The albums that were now made were brimming with Icelandic cultural references as well as subtle but hard-hitting left-wing critique laden with cynical humour. The canon produced by these three college bands is wonderfully indefinable – funny and surreal but simultaneously serious and political as it plunges into the nation's psyche and comes up with a unique, inimitable form of Icelandic popular music.

The roots of Stuðmenn lie in two friends, Valgeir Guðjónsson and Jakob Frímann Magnússon, who went for the corniest band name they could think of, to counter the all-prevailing musical seriousness around them.[21] Dressed in attire worn by 1950s hipsters, considered very passé at the time, they went down well at their debut concert. The project was therefore brought out again for future endeavours although few could have predicted that this band would become Iceland's biggest band, capable of bridging generations. In 1974 an Icelandic entrepreneur, Ámundi Ámundason, offered Valgeir and Jakob the chance to record two singles, which were speedily released. Valgeir, who had begun more serious musicianship with Spilverk þjóðanna, flew to London as Jakob had been touring around the UK playing Hammond organ with Long John Baldry's band. The pair hired Cliff Richard's rhythm section to record the singles and a whole album was recorded a year later in London, the city that had proven so important when Icelandic musicians wanted to take things up a notch.[22] This time around, Valgeir brought along his mates from Spilverkið, Jakob called on famous friends like Chris Spedding, Bill Bruford and Long John Baldry, and Björgvin Halldórsson, who was waiting for world fame with Change, provided some vocals.[23]

The resulting album, released in 1975, was called *Sumar á Sýrlandi* (Summer in Syria, but could also be interpreted, given some of the themes addressed on the album, as 'Summer in Acid-Land'; Acid = *Sýra*). The album would prove to be a momentous event in Icelandic popular music history. The band were wont to do things tongue-in-cheek, playing with double entendres, and the album was full of fun and surrealism. Poignant thoughts on the realities of Icelanders bubbled under the surface as well. Musically, it was diverse, almost like a commentary on the styles that the members had been toying with in their youth. The album is also a conceptual ride, in fact a knowing play on the 'concept' of the concept album, and the band somehow managed to keep a cool distance without sacrificing their authenticity. The album's story is shown as a cartoon on the back of the cover, where we follow a few friends on a mind-bending road trip. It starts out innocently enough, with our hero, soda bottle in hand, waiting for his friends at a bus stop. They start partying freely, all in 1950s regalia, and side one closes with a track where the gang enters a 'blue shadow', a thinly veiled reference to marijuana smoking. Come side two, they are 'flying' to the spirit world and at the album's close our protagonist wakes up from a dream – still at the bus stop.

The album was an instant classic in Iceland, its legendary status intact ever since; in many ways, it was a crossover success, offering

Stuðmenn's debut album *Sumar á Sýrlandi* (1975) created quite a stir upon its release and has maintained a classic status among the Icelandic listening public.

plenty for both the intelligentsia and the casual pop fan. Critics hailed the album and talked about a fresh, all-Icelandic tone. The critic for *Morgunblaðið* at the time, Ómar Valdimarsson, said: 'In my view, it's one of the most interesting and important rock albums to have been released in this country. Stuðmenn are probably right, that their music is an all-Icelandic rock. But I'm very unsure if the contents will translate to the public.'[24] His last proclamation proved to be way off the mark.

Stuðmenn promoted the album in Iceland, hiding their identities with costumes and masks, referencing old popular culture and the made-up band that 'played' on *Sgt. Pepper's Lonely Hearts*

Club Band. The album is also noteworthy for the fact that it was the first release by future record mogul Steinar Berg Ísleifsson, who released it through his Egg imprint. Later, the 'Steinar' label would be the biggest mainstream label in Iceland, alongside Skífan (interestingly, Skífan's future owner, Jón Ólafsson (not to be confused with the musician mentioned in the book), also battled for the release of this one Stuðmenn album at the time, though it remains unclear which imprint it was intended for).[25] Much later, and after various wranglings, Steinar and Skífan would end up as Sena, in reality the only Icelandic label that could be considered a 'major' and the owner of most of the back catalogue of Icelandic music (the music sector of Sena and its catalogue is now run as Alda Music).

A new Stuðmenn album, *Tivoli* (Amusement Park), appeared a year later. Again, *Sgt. Pepper*-era Beatles proved an influence, lyrically at least, as most of the songs were steeped in nostalgic reminiscences about the members' youth (think 'Strawberry Fields Forever' and 'Penny Lane'). *Sumar á Sýrlandi* had dealt with the bandmates' teenage years, but on the second album an amusement park that had been in operation in Reykjavík when the members were kids was the focal point. The music was more refined this time around but no less impressive. Soon after the release, various members became occupied with other projects and Stuðmenn was put on hold, before making a massive comeback at the start of the 1980s.

Spilverk þjóðanna, the preoccupation of Valgeir, Egill Ólafsson and the enigmatic Sigurður Bjóla (the 'lost' genius of Icelandic popular music), had been run alongside Stuðmenn. Although playing regularly since 1972 and slowly building a fan base, their debut wasn't released until three years later (coincidentally, the same year as *Sumar á Sýrlandi*). By that time, songstress Diddú had been added to the fold. It was recorded at Hljóðriti and contains restrained folk music, an amalgam of British, American and Scandinavian styles. The second album, *CD Nærlífi* (CD Nearlife), released in 1976, was recorded live at Hljóðriti in front of an audience.[26] Similarly styled and with English lyrics just like the debut, these albums are quite basic in hindsight and rarely hint at the glories that lay ahead. If those two albums had been the only ones that the group made, they would merely be an interesting footnote in Icelandic pop music history. But Spilverkið took their music to another level on their third album, *Götuskór* (Town Shoes), also released in 1976. A concept album (but of course) following the adventures of a paper boy sung in Icelandic. *Sturla*, the band's fourth album, released in 1977, is for many the band's pinnacle, highlighting the advantages of their shift in language. Very 'Icelandic', the album's name is an old male name from the Viking age, and the cover depicts Icelandicness, with its rural romanticism, featuring a horse, an old, battered car and some laundry hanging from a clothesline. The album itself brims with Icelandic cultural references and a certain 1970s Icelandic ambiance is palpable. But most importantly it's laced with unabashed creative joy that's positively affecting. After its release, Egill left to focus on his new band, Hinn íslenzki þursaflokkur. Spilverkið soldiered on as a trio, augmented by session musicians, and could do nothing wrong, releasing two strong albums before the band folded in 1979. The 1978 album was aptly called *Ísland* (Iceland), the cover featuring the members looking up at the camera from a floating replica of the country, which had been placed in Reykjavíkurtjörn (Reykjavík's pond) in the city centre. The band's final statement, released in 1979, is called *Bráðabirgðabúgí* (Temporary Boogie) and manages to eclipse *Sturla* in greatness, drawing on every strength that had made this band so distinctive. The tried-and-tested concept album was elegantly put to use this time around, detailing a rural couple who move to the 'big' city, Reykjavík, and the hardships that face them there. The songs are socio-realistic vignettes with powerful, insightful lyrics that hold a mirror to Icelandic society at the end of the 1970s, where the rat race often got the better of people.

The album manages to paint a vivid picture of the drab, grey Reykjavík as it was at the end of the 1970s. The city was clawing its way into modernity; for instance, the first shopping mall escalator was nothing less than headline news, with people making the trip to try it out. Mostly, Reykjavík was an unremarkable, small city (*c.* 100,000 inhabitants) in a former Danish colony. To this day, there is one modest high street (Laugavegur) with small side streets. In the centre, there are two small squares, not far from the pond just mentioned. The live venues in Reykjavík are to be found in Laugavegur and near the squares, as is Reykjavík's nightlife. The punk scene was partly nurtured at Hótel Borg, an Art Deco hotel that opened in the pivotal year of 1930, located just across from the parliament building by Austurvöllur public square. This square was also home to NASA, the city's most renowned concert venue in the 2000s, which closed in 2012. A few blocks away is Gaukurinn, also known as Gaukur á Stöng, a famous concert venue that has been operating since 1983. The harbour is also close by, where The Sugarcubes had their first practice space. Much of the story told in these pages unfolded within these few square kilometres. 'Is that

Gaukurinn, or Gaukur á Stöng, is a long-running concert venue and a rock institution, located in downtown Reykjavík.

it?' remarked one bewildered tourist in the 2000s when he found himself in the city centre.

Spilverkið were without a doubt at the top of the folk-pop/rock hierarchy, but the decade saw more similar bands of note, contributing to a home-brewed version of the 1970s folk strand. The acutely political Þokkabót released some fine albums with socially aware, Icelandic lyrics, and are best known for their cover of Pete Seeger's 'Little Boxes'.[27] Bands like Melchior and Diabolus In Musica also chipped in with folky chamber-pop. Þrjú á palli (Three on a Stage) had also been very active at the beginning of the 1970s, releasing a much-heralded Christmas album in 1971 for which the members arranged some century-old Icelandic folk songs. Hörður Torfason, mentioned briefly at the end of the preceding chapter, released an album in 1970, *Hörður Torfason syngur eigin lög* (Hörður Torfason Sings His Own Songs) on SG-Records, comprising Icelandic poems set to his own folk-styled compositions. The album was a great success and set Hörður on a fruitful path; his deviant, independent spirit influencing many a soul. Alongside theatre work, Hörður continues to release albums and plays concerts regularly. Hörður was the first openly gay man in Iceland, and he was a leading light in gay activism for many decades. In keeping with his fighting spirit, Hörður was the instigator of the Icelandic 'Pots and Pans Revolution', born out of the financial crisis that hit the country in autumn 2008. Staging a one-man protest in October that year in front of the Icelandic parliament building, the protests built up gradually, culminating in riots on 20 January 2009, effectively putting the Icelandic government out of office in April. Demonstrators banged pots long into the night and the local press referred to the events as the Kitchenware Revolution (*Búsáhaldabyltingin*), more commonly known as the 'Pots and Pans Revolution'.[28]

Egill Ólafsson, former Spilverkið and Stuðmenn member, headed for similar pastures to Þrjú á palli with his new band, Þursaflokkurinn. It's remarkable in itself that colourful characters like Egill, Valgeir and Jakob could be in the same band at one time, kind of like The Beatles operating with three Lennons among their ranks. Jakob was by now busy with his solo career, having recorded an album in 1976, his charisma and connections luring Phil Collins to the drum stool. Egill, on the other hand, went further inland, so to speak, his new band wholly devoted to the musical heritage of Iceland, rather than British, American or the other Scandinavian countries. Egill had been studying the Icelandic Folksongs collection amassed by the Rev. Bjarni Þorsteinsson and wanted to utilize it in a modern setting. Some of these songs were introduced on the band's debut album, simply called *Hinn íslenzki þursaflokkur*, released in late 1978. The music was folky prog rock, not unlike what Jethro Tull had been doing on their most recent albums, *Songs from the Wood* (1977) and *Heavy Horses* (1978) and the opening track justly reminded people of the Dutch band Focus and their best-known song, 'Hocus Pocus'. The lyrics were, naturally, all in Icelandic, succinctly phrased and beautifully sung by the multitalented Egill. The arrangements and instrumentation (the group had a bassoon player) betrayed a distinctive air of medievalism. As with the other two units from the college trinity Stuðmenn and Spilverk þjóðanna, there was something very Icelandic about Þursaflokkurinn and not only because of the music utilized. The album became very popular, like the band, who had been gigging relentlessly since forming at the beginning of 1978. The next album, *Þursabit* (Lumbago, 1979) built on the predecessor but introduced jazzy, heavier prog leanings, courtesy of Karl Sighvatsson, the veteran and virtuoso from Trúbrot/Náttúra. This perfectly realized vision of Þursaflokkurinn, merging the ancient and the modern, was then symbolically played out in a concert at the National Theatre of Iceland in 1980, a most important cultural institution in the minds of Icelanders, as it was founded early in the wake of the country's hard-won independence. The band was the first rock band to play in the theatre and an accompanying live album was released the same year, *Á hljómleikum* (In Concert).[29]

The band survived the 1970s with grace, releasing their final album in 1982 and playing their last shows in 1984. Their swansong, *Gœti eins verið* (Could As Well Be), was yet another quality affair, an impressive response to the changing soundscapes in the rock world. The album is wholly unique, weird yet accessible and combines prog rock and new wave sensibilities with remarkable ease. Work began on a fourth album that remains unreleased, although five tracks saw the light of day in a box set released in 2008. The music there is simply miraculous. Alongside prog and New Romantic elements, there's ambient jazz and world music touches. It shouldn't work, but somehow it does.

Þursaflokkurinn packed it in for various reasons. Acrimony was not a part of it, the members were simply tired of slaving away for little, if any, financial return. The revival of Stuðmenn, which shared members with Þursaflokkurinn, was also beginning to get wind in its sails. A lack of interest from abroad also played its part; playing the same clubs and for the same audience is tiresome and 'the village' can be suffocating for aspiring, ambitious musicians. Lest we forget

Hinn íslenzki þursaflokkur blended rock with Icelandic folk music and are held in high regard to this day. This photo is a still from the film *Rokk í Reykjavík* (1982).

and as has been told, 1970s and '80s Iceland was still more or less a remote and uninteresting place; the tourist industry as we know it today, with its emphasis on nature, was pretty much non-existent. Þursaflokkurinn was revived in 2007 for a concert, played with the Icelandic contemporary music ensemble Caput in February 2008, marking the 30th anniversary of the band, and played some more concerts in the aftermath. Egill still maintains that the band did not come to full fruition in the 1980s although no plans have been set for rectifying that situation.[30]

The conglomerate creative forces were at an all-time high in 1977 when Valgeir teamed up with a friend, Leifur Hauksson from Þokkabót, to record a socially aware and quite leftist children's record. The project was given the name *Hrekkjusvín* (Rascals) and the album, *Lög unga fólksins* (The Songs of the Young People), bore the musical streak of both Spilverkið and Þokkabót. The record bustles and brims with excitement and energy, and everything that these musicians touched seemed to turn to gold. The album remains a classic and its strength has a lot to do with the pointed lyrics, written by author Pétur Gunnarsson. They scorch through society's ailments, armed with sheer bravado and humour, offering a pointed commentary on Icelandic society in the late 1970s, just like Spilverkið did on their later albums.

The legacy of the three interlocked bands, Stuðmenn, Spilverkið and Þursaflokkurinn, still resounds with Icelandic music and culture in general and in the most recent poll on Iceland's greatest albums, which was an elaborate book project (*100 bestu plötur Íslandssögunnar*, The 100 Greatest Icelandic Albums of All Time) the bands are responsible for four albums in the top ten.[31] For the first time, Icelandicness was used as the springboard for art-making rather than roping in influences from afar. All of the bands did this in their distinctive way, Stuðmenn with Icelandic humour, Spilverkið with Icelandic social realism and Þursaflokkurinn with Icelandic folk music and lore. And funnily enough, that stance would prove fruitful in the years to come, although it did not reap any rewards at the time. Similar developments were taking place in other Scandinavian countries: bands infusing their respective folk heritage into rock music and dipping into their social surroundings for lyrical inspiration. These moves represented a rebellion of sorts against the Anglo-American cultural tycoons who had ruled the 1950s and '60s. In Iceland this manifested itself in four ways: the use of Icelandic heritage; humour; social reality; and folk music. A unique Icelandic take on the universal aspects of pop and rock was thus born in the 1970s.

Icelandic artists and bands that have made it in seismic fashion have followed a similar trajectory, letting go of preconceived notions about how to succeed and instead just doing their own thing, without any strategy or long-term planning. The Sugarcubes were founded as a prank when their core members gave up on their former band, Kukl, a serious post-punk endeavour in the mould of Crass, the English anarcho-punk band/collective of the late 1970s–80s. Björk, with a gleam in her eyes, said in a 1990 interview with *Morgunblaðið* that she was generally surprised by the fact that people weren't crying in front of the stage when Kukl played.[32] The Sugarcubes, on the other hand, were formed as an in-joke, a big contrast to the seriousness of Kukl. The mission was to fool around with every pop cliché in the book and that strategy backfired beautifully of course. Similarly, Sigur Rós, neo-hippies one and all, had no inkling that anyone outside of their close-knit underground listeners would care for their music.

This decade also introduced an important figure whose enigmatic presence has loomed large over Icelandic pop music ever since. Magnús Þór Jónsson – or Megas as he is artistically known – came out of nowhere in 1972 with an eponymous debut album and, like the three bands already detailed, his contribution to Icelandic music and culture is incalculable.[33] The 'Icelandic Bob Dylan' tag is no coincidence.

Megas was and is a certified bohemian and had published some poetry in college. Able to read music (he played piano at a young age), he published some lyrics and songs as sheet music at the end of the 1960s. The eponymous record was released in limited quantity (650 copies) and was a watershed. The music was acoustic, folky singer-songwriter stuff, sung in a nasal (many said ugly) manner, just like Dylan. But the real shock came when people listened to the lyrics. Historical Icelandic figures, many of them venerated and with sacred status, were attacked with humorous, satiric glee. Some of the songs were banned from the radio due to their subject matter; in one of them Megas wishes that the ship of Ingólfur Arnarson, who was the first permanent Nordic settler in Iceland, had sunk and bemoans his unfortunate serendipity. Left-leaning artists and the intelligentsia were quick to proclaim him a genius and a saviour while the conservatives poured scorn on Megas. Little has changed in those matters to this day. But even his staunchest enemies would find it difficult to deny his rich contribution to the Icelandic language.

Megas continued with similar lyrical themes on his next album, *Millilending* (Stopover), released three years later (and recorded in Hljóðriti). This time around he enjoyed a rock band setting and one of the reasons was that he wanted to emulate the 'going electric' antics of Dylan.[34] But a more deep-seated reason was that his first love was rock 'n' roll, Presley and the like, and that was the musical route he wanted to take initially. The band that provided the backing was Júdas, a popular rock band at the time.[35] On his third album, *Fram og aftur blindgötuna* (Back and Forth on a Dead-End Street), released a year later, in 1976, he yet again used rock musicians (members from the bands Celsius and Eik respectively).[36] Megas continued with his lambasting of all things sacred and the albums gradually became darker in tone. A look at how Megas's cover artworks developed is revealing in this respect. The debut is adorned with a nonchalant black-and-white picture of the artist, standard for singer-songwriters at the time. On the second one, Megas sits by a grey concrete wall, holding small yellow flowers, and a certain contempt cuts through the hippyish photo. Things are taken up a notch

– and then some – on the third album. Not only does the title imply some shadowy dealings but by a table adorned with flowers and a white bust of Beethoven sits a gaunt and grim Megas, wearing a leather jacket and clutching a whip. His stare piercing, merciless.

Megas became a very controversial figure around this time. He fanned the flames, subconsciously or not, appearing for instance in a television interview with a patch on one eye, resembling a rough and ready pirate. The music flowed out of him as well and the quality – and the revolutionary stance – was astonishing. *Fram og aftur blindgötuna* is often singled out as Megas's masterpiece and a year later (1977) he managed another one, this time in collaboration with Spilverk þjóðanna. The album, *Á bleikum náttkjólum* (In Pink Nightgowns), is revered to this day as one of the greatest Icelandic albums ever made. A year after that, it was time for a children's record, the eerie *Nú er ég klæddur og kominn á ról* (Now I'm Dressed and Up and About). Megas delved into Icelandic lullabies and children's songs, accompanied by classical instrumentation, showing both an acute knowledge of the heritage and a masterful and wholly different take on the material. It really is a frightening listen (the fourth movement is called 'Grave Horrible/Allegro').

Megas's deep knowledge of Icelandic cultural heritage was also displayed shortly after his debut album. He composed fifty original tunes for The Hymns of the Passion and performed them in a concert; a collection of fifty hymns to be sung, one each working day, during the seven weeks of Lent. The hymns were composed by the poet and minister Hallgrímur Pétursson in the seventeenth century and resound deeply within the Icelandic psyche. They are broadcast every Easter on national radio, read by different cultural luminaries. In this instance, Megas approached the material with the utmost respect although this was, of course, considered a sacrilege. 'There was a lot of respect for the hymns in the household when I was growing up,' Megas remembered in 2001. 'And one of the rules was not to turn down the radio when they were on. So, I learnt them all

The cover of Megas's third album, *Fram og aftur blindgötuna* (1976), features this striking image of Icelandic popular music's *enfant terrible*.

whether I liked it or not. When I came of age, I started to find curious and strange things in them and that spurred me on.'[37]

Megas bid farewell to the decade with a double live album of original material, some of it dating back to the sheet music he had published in the 1960s. Rumours about his gargantuan drug intake were rife and the title of the album, *Drög að sjálfsmorði* (Drafts for Suicide), did little to put them to rest and implied that the musician was about to bid us farewell for good. On the cover, Megas holds a messianic pose, with a slight, manic grin, and the title and the symbolism led to an official statement from Megas where he proclaimed that he was, contrary to rumours, alive and kicking. Megas then disappeared from sight, only to re-emerge in the mid-1980s.

Few Icelandic artists have contributed so richly to the Icelandic language by showing its possibilities for meaning, bite and value in the context of popular music. Megas was awarded the Jónas Hallgrímsson prize, an Icelandic language award, in 2000 on the annual 'Icelandic Language Day' (16 November, the birthday of said Jónas, Iceland's best-loved poet). The award is given to individuals who have 'worked in favour of the language through writing or speaking, in fiction, studies or teaching, and worked for its enrichment, advancement and passing down to younger generations'. A TV reporter asked Megas what receiving the prize meant to him. Ever the cynic, Megas answered drearily in English 'Bunch of money.'[38]

Some songs from *Á bleikum náttkjólum*, Megas's collaboration with Spilverk þjóðanna, hint at the unruly punk scene that was just around the corner. 'Paradísarfuglinn' contains an angular and gritty guitar riff, punky if not consciously punk. Þursaflokkurinn responded to the times ahead in a similar fashion, finishing off their 1980 live album with a raw punk song, built on an old sea shanty in line with their interest in Icelandic folklore. Some of the members had seen the Sex Pistols play in London and although fairly unimpressed with the music they couldn't deny the energy that filled the concert hall.[39]

As elsewhere, musicians from the 1970s had difficulty finding their feet in the punk era and many were made redundant overnight. The conglomerate managed to adapt somewhat but one artist had unquestioned adulation from the punk crowd, namely Megas. A spiritual grandfather of sorts, his rebellious nature and refreshing lack of respect for what can be done and what not in terms of a shared, Icelandic heritage inspired the punk generation.

4

The 1980s: Punk Emerges and The Sugarcubes Break the Chain

'"The professional rock music," Thór [of The Sugarcubes] says with a dismissive sniff, "what it lacks is vitality, the lust for life. We have that in abundance. We are in harmony with life itself." Welcome to Iceland – pop's last frontier. For real.'[1]

Punk rock made quite an impact in Iceland, just like everywhere else. After an unusually long gestation time, punk exploded in the winter of 1981–2 when every other garage was filled with wide-eyed upstarts, galvanized by a liberating DIY attitude, getting their bands off the ground.[2] Visits from big names such as The Stranglers and The Clash (who played here in 1978 and 1980 respectively) had been influential, both playing in the Laugardalshöll sports arena (just as Led Zeppelin had previously). Indeed, that arena was for a long time the only place in Iceland where foreign acts of considerable size played (the culture of one, indeed).

The punk upheaval was documented in the legendary film *Rokk í Reykjavík* (Rock in Reykjavík), released in April 1982 and one of the most lauded films in Icelandic history.[3] The director, Friðrik Þór Friðriksson, went on to become one of Iceland's most prolific and respected directors (his film *Börn náttúrunnar* or Children of Nature (1991) is the only Icelandic film to have been nominated for an Oscar, when it was nominated as the Best Foreign Language Film). *Rokk í Reykjavík* was widely circulated on videocassette in the 1980s and instantly garnered cult status. It became quite influential, in many ways informing and inspiring later scenes such as the indie rock boom at the start of the 1990s. Because of the delayed arrival of punk to Iceland – post-punk was firmly established by that time in most other countries – the period was characterized by a weird combination of styles where almost all strands of punk/new wave music up to that time were squeezed into one compact package. Ramones-style punk-by-numbers, new wave inklings, 1970s-inspired metal and pub rock rubbed shoulders with New Romantics, post-punkers, hardcore groups and experimentalists.

In countless interviews with British beat groups, punk groups, heavy metal bands and so on, band members often give an account of the sheer desperation that initially drove them to make music. The music was a way out; out of the factory, out of the office and out of the pie shop that your father was running. A calling, yes, but also an escape. The immobility in terms of social strata in the UK plays a big part in its music history, its palpability egging on talented working-class band members.[4] Similar accounts are not to be found in Iceland. People formed bands as a side thing, for the fun of it, with the notion that if it didn't work out they would simply move on to something else. The be-all/end-all factor is non-existent when Icelandic popular musicians reminisce about their beginnings in the industry, in part guided by the relative classless reality Icelanders enjoyed after the Second World War and long into the twentieth century (this does not apply today, I'm afraid).

So, Icelandic historians and sociologists have scratched their heads over the 'punk delay'. Why have other scenes, original rock 'n' roll, death metal, for example, followed foreign developments quite closely while punk did not? One explanation is that the economy in Iceland at the end of the 1970s was simply too healthy. While unemployment and mounting disaffection spurred the UK punk scene on, nothing of that sort – or at least not on a big enough scale – was happening here. In other words, the Icelandic youth was simply too materially comfortable to tap into the alienation of punk.[5] When punk finally arrived, it was not – at least not exclusively – shaped by political motivation and social alienation but rather the artistic freedom and DIY spirit that came with it.[6] The individual's power to make something for themselves and at the same time parting with the musical dinosaurs that had prevailed in the 1970s was enticing to Icelandic youth and adventurous musicians. The prevailing spirit of optimism, all-around activity and communal brother and sisterhood was in many ways at odds with the pessimism and darkness that characterized some of the more popular punk and post-punk groups from the UK, which most of the Icelandic bands nonetheless looked to for inspiration.[7]

It's also tempting to attribute the oddness of the Icelandic punk explosion to known Icelandic national characteristics, where things tend to be executed quickly and hazily but nonetheless quite efficiently. Operations in this small society are often guided by the very Icelandic phrase *þetta reddast* or 'it will be OK – somehow!'[8] In the case of Icelandic punk, it was like our music culture was abruptly reminded of the fact that punk had slipped through its fingers, resulting in a collective team effort to get things done and then herding four years' worth of punk culture history into one brazen winter of activities. This theory is light-hearted, mind you, but not without merit, given this author's experience on the ground with Icelandic culture and especially the music culture.[9]

The first real Icelandic punk band was Fræbbblarnir (The Staaamens). The band was formed in 1978 in Kópavogur, the second largest municipality in Iceland, with the grand total of 39,335 inhabitants.[10] The town would spawn quite a number of eligible punk bands and quickly became a stronghold for grassroots concerts, hosting many revolutionary gigs in the town's old cinema hall. Fræbbblarnir had been formed as a one-off joke by college students, determined to trick the headmaster with heaps of horrible noise (playing Sex Pistols songs with Icelandic lyrics). Later on they released original music, snappy Ramones-inspired material, with clever and funny lyrics; sometimes political, sometimes filled with everyday observations.

Fræbbblarnir were active on the live front in 1979, just about the only band of its type, although some very short-lived combos made appearances as well. The band did not manage to put a record out until 1980, when an indie label from Sheffield released a three-track 7-inch single. An album followed later that year. As I've described, things moved quite slowly on the Icelandic punk front compared to its places of origin, the UK and the USA. Stray visionaries blew their trumpets, bringing records home from London and playing them for similarly minded friends. Einar Örn Benediktsson, later of The Sugarcubes, was one of those pioneers, as he was living with his parents in London around 1977. He was one of the first to adopt the punk look; frizzy hair, badges and chains, and stood out memorably in his class photo, taken in spring 1978.[11] Einar would later form Purrkur Pillnikk, a seminal Icelandic punk band.

Fræbbblarnir were the harbingers but the first real stars were Utangarðsmenn, whose name translates into English as The Outsiders, although the literal meaning is 'men outside the garden', that is, 'avant-garde', adhering to those on society's fringes. Utangarðsmenn kicked into gear in 1980 and quickly became the reigning kings of the Icelandic punk wave, playing fast, punk-infused R&B with socially aware lyrics. The band was led by the indomitable and highly charismatic Bubbi Morthens. 'Bubbi' – as he is known colloquially – would subsequently become a highly significant figure in Icelandic pop and rock. A Joe Strummer type of sorts (add a healthy dose of Bragg/Springsteen/Dylan into the mix), Bubbi travelled around the country at the start of the 1970s, working in fisheries and the like, sometimes playing his Woody Guthrie-inspired songs for fellow workers. As the decade progressed he began performing live at political gatherings and at events organized by an Icelandic folk/traditional music society (Vísnavinir, literally 'friends of verse'), winning praise for his singing and stage charisma.[12] His self-funded debut LP *Ísbjarnarblús* (Polar Bear Blues, 1980) was initially intended to be an acoustic album with politically charged protest songs but after striking up a friendship with two guitar-slinging brothers, Mike and Danny Pollock, some punk songs slipped in as well.[13] Utangarðsmenn were born shortly after and burned brightly in 1980, opening for The Clash in Laugardalshöll arena, another landmark event like The Stranglers concert two years before.

Everything was in full motion in 1981/2, as made clear in the *Rokk í Reykjavík* documentary. Since its release, the film has been the main source of knowledge about Icelandic punk and for a long time almost the only source. Bands that weren't in the film (or on

Bubbi Morthens's debut album, *Ísbjarnarblús* (1980). His status in Icelandic popular music culture is absolutely unique.

Purrkur Pillnikk did a lot, did it fast and did it brilliantly in the heyday of Icelandic punk.

its accompanying album) were almost wholly forgotten as a result. Renewed interest in the period, along with the wonders of the Internet, has fortunately rectified this. Many of Iceland's most influential musicians took their first steps during this time. Tappi Tíkarrass (Cork Bitch's Ass) was Björk's first foray into punk music.[14] She was fifteen when the band started and the music was vigorous, a fun-filled cross between punk and new wave. Purrkur Pillnikk, with Einar Örn on vocals, had a short but very active lifespan; a lot of records and concerts, and the music was fast and furious, spiky, angular punk with brilliantly poignant lyrics delivered in manic style by the unstoppable life force that Einar embodied at this time.[15] In record time, they progressed from simple, endearing punk songwriting to a more developed sound, not unlike Gang of Four and Wire's more experimental stuff. Q4U were also brilliant, with the undeniable swagger of singer Ellý and bassist Gunnþór.

As already explained, Iceland's punk scene was like a showcase of punk's development from 1976 to 1981 and the occult-dabbling Þeyr carried the torch of doom and gloom, inspired by Joy Division and Killing Joke. The band featured one Sigtryggur Baldursson on drums (later of The Sugarcubes) and the guitar player Godkrist (Guðlaugur Kristinn Óttarsson), later of pre-Sugarcubes band Kukl. The mighty Þeyr was a phenomenal band, with a unique aura, and its development from 1979 to 1983 was remarkable. The output towards the end sailed easily alongside similar, better-known post-punk bands from the UK, especially with regard to Killing Joke, and the band struck up a friendship with its singer, Jaz Coleman (Coleman moved to Iceland in 1983 with his guitarist, Kevin 'Geordie' Walker, forming a band with Þeyr members called Iceland). Þeyr would prove influential and were an important reference point for young underground musicians in the early 1990s who had been reared on worn-out VHS copies of *Rokk í Reykjavík*.

The punk scene was almost squarely positioned in the capital area. The most glaring exception was the superb Bara flokkurinn (The 'Just Because' Group) from Akureyri, the capital of the north and Iceland's biggest rural town (population just under 20,000 today but around 13,000 in 1982). Bara flokkurinn released three strong records, a six-track EP and two LPS, getting progressively better with each release. The band grew quickly from chimerical new wave guitar rock to sophisticated New Romantic pop à la Ultravox, its maturity and tightness on the last record (*Gas*, 1983) a marvel to behold. But like so many of the artists already mentioned, the lack of access to bigger markets made them a local concern at best.[16]

Before we leave the Icelandic punk scene, I have to mention Grýlurnar (The Witches), an all-female band formed by Ragnhildur Gísladóttir, who had been a part of the pop scene since the late 1970s. Grýlurnar were established both as an artistic outlet (the music was weird, left-of-centre new wave) and as a call to arms for women to participate in the new music scene, which was dominated by men. Grýlurnar partook in *Rokk í Reykjavík* and their 'just do it' message to women was clear and resounding. Dúkkulísur (Paper Dolls) from the Eastfjords were taking notes. Formed in 1982, the following year they competed in a Battle of the Bands competition, Músíktilraunir (see later in this chapter), and won. A great band with a bit of a Bangles feel to it, they released two albums, two songs from which became radio hits (including the rallying feminist cry 'Pamela'). The band is still active.

By autumn 1981 Bubbi had split from Utangarðsmenn, who soldiered on as Bodies. Bubbi formed a new group, Egó (as a self-referential joke). Utangarðsmenn had only mustered one LP before they imploded but Egó racked up three before calling it quits in 1984. Bubbi had become a superstar overnight at the start of the 1980s and his work rate in that decade was incredible. It has continued unabated to this day and Bubbi has released around 75 albums, over 50 of them solo and the rest through groups or collaborations. A prime example of a 'non-exportable' Icelandic musician, he's unequalled in terms of the impact he had at the time, an opinionated,

Grýlurnar brought with them some much-needed feminine empowerment at the start of the 1980s.

charismatic loudmouth and a larger-than-life figure whose music is known and loved by generations (similar to the status enjoyed by Kim Larsen in Denmark or Udo Lindenberg in Germany). Almost a complete unknown to the outside world, Bubbi is a king in his own country (and he is indeed often referred to as 'The King'). Bubbi's songs are buried in the psyche of Icelanders of a certain generation who can sing along to a few dozen of his songs, whether they like it or not. His lyrics – all in Icelandic – spoke to the everyman and his brashness towards taboo topics is something to applaud (his 2019 album *Regnbogans stræti* (Rainbow Street) opens with a song welcoming immigrants from war-torn areas).

In 1985 Bubbi went to a rehab centre. That year's album, *Kona* (Woman), brought a notable change, taking on a sombre and introverted tone, often regarded as his career zenith. Fame- and sales-wise he went into overdrive after the mid-1980s – his albums usually sold around 30,000 copies, a lot when the total population is 250,000. During this time, efforts were made to market Bubbi outside of Iceland. A Swedish label (Mistlur) released an album in English (*Serbian Flower*, 1988) but it did not stick and Bubbi's fate as an Icelandic performer first and foremost was sealed. And on Icelandic soil, no one came close to his iconic status. In poppy troubadour terms we could name Bjartmar Guðlaugsson, who played homely music infused with clever, relatable lyrics. His humorous detailing of the drabness of everyday life together with his gift for melodies made him an unlikely star for a brief time in the late 1980s.

The punk scene started to fold shortly after *Rokk í Reykjavík* debuted and 1983–4 was a sort of interval time. In 1981 Ásmundur Jónsson established the label and record shop Gramm or Grammið alongside punk purveyors like Einar Örn from Purrkur Pillnikk. Grammið would morph into Bad Taste (Smekkleysa SM ehf in Icelandic) in 1986, the label that would release The Sugarcubes' first record. Ásmundur or Ási, who would become Bad Taste's managing director, had by then over ten years' worth of experience working in the music industry at large, starting out as a music journalist, a radio personality and a record store clerk. He gradually moved into gig promotion and artist management alongside running the Grammið label and store.[17] One of Ásmundur's key contributions to the Icelandic punk scene and later the underground/art rock scene lies in the radio programme *Áfangar* (Stages, or Phases), which he co-hosted with Guðni Rúnar Agnarsson in the years 1973–83 on national radio (then the only radio station in the country). The programme is now part of musical folklore; in the style of John Peel, the two colleagues played music not often heard on the radio, and original listeners recall the show with a sense of bleary-eyed nostalgia.

It was in that programme's final show, in summer 1983, that the seeds for Bad Taste were sown. In that particular episode, Ásmundur and Guðni called up a few of their favourite musicians and got them to play together. The band Kukl was established and in its ranks were future Sugarcubes Björk, Einar Örn, Einar Melax and Sigtryggur Baldursson alongside Guðlaugur 'Godkrist' Óttarsson (of Þeyr fame) and Birgir Mogensen, bass player from Spilafífl (Playing Fools). Kukl was thus a punk supergroup that would eventually evolve into The Sugarcubes.[18] Kukl's music was powerful and intense – arty, heavy, progressive and 'difficult'. The band had connections to the UK anarcho-punk scene: Einar was friends with Flux of Pink Indians' bassist, Derek Birkett, and had played trumpet with the band while seeking his journalism degree in London. As it was, the two Kukl albums were released by Crass Records, *The Eye* in 1984 and *Holidays in Europe* in 1986, the latter produced by Crass's Penny Rimbaud.

Those in the know, home and abroad, were highly impressed by the band's music but the general public in Iceland didn't care and dismissed it as indecipherable nonsense. When the members switched gears and lightened up in the 'pop' group The Sugarcubes, it soon became the year zero in terms of substantive foreign interest in Icelandic popular music. A band with a sustainable career, media interest, international distribution and fan following – a basic popular music industry trajectory that lasted a few years (six years, to be exact). We will decipher this more closely later in the chapter. To recap, in the 1980s, the connections to the mainstream pop world were strengthening and a platform for real and substantial undertakings was slowly being built. But the first big exposure to Icelandic music in the Anglo-American pop/rock world happened three years before The Sugarcubes were formed, through a band that was as far removed from the fertile punk scene as possible. Mezzoforte had been releasing fusion albums domestically since the late 1970s, playing for a small but receptive audience, and was made up of implausibly young members. The band was started in 1977 by fourteen- and sixteen-year-olds, playing complex jazz-fusion patterns inspired by Weather Report and Return to Forever.

In 1983 Mezzoforte's song 'Garden Party' made it to number seventeen on the Official UK Top 40 Chart, an achievement not bettered until ten years later, when Björk's 'Play Dead' (featuring David Arnold) made it to number twelve.[19] Mezzoforte's chart entry put Icelandic society into hyperdrive and their label manager, Steinar Berg (the same guy who had released Stuðmenn in the 1970s), established an office in London in order to pursue world fame. This event is firmly in the annals of Icelandic history, regularly discussed and digested, and we still revel in this the-little-guys-who-could success story. Just like the few medals we've won at the Olympics. When you live in a little 'village', these things count.[20] Although world fame eluded the group, Icelanders hold the band in high regard, as does the international fusion scene, and Mezzoforte tour quite regularly, with a loyal fan base that extends to Scandinavia, Eastern Europe and Asia.[21]

The same year as *Rokk í Reykjavík* had its debut screening, Stuðmenn released an off-the-cuff musical road movie called *Með allt á hreinu*, or *On Top*, as it was titled outside of Iceland (the phrase *ég er með allt á hreinu* means 'I'm on top of things'). Released at the height of punk, the music contained within had little to do with punk's raw racket. The plot (scripted overnight by Stuðmenn's keyboard player and all-round Svengali Jakob Frímann Magnússon) revolves around two warring bands, Stuðmenn and the all-female Grýlurnar (called Gærurnar in the film – a derogatory term meaning tarts/sluts). The bands drive around the country in separate buses, playing empty halls and having run-ins, and the storyline, with whole scenes sometimes improvised on the spot, has room for all kinds of shenanigans, cheap jokes and, of course, regular musical numbers. On the surface, the film might seem light and superficial, but it runs deeper than that. There's a keen commentary on Icelandic customs and attitudes throughout but there's also a feminist critique, held aloft by Grýlurnar, who were making an impact in the Icelandic punk scene at the time, often explicitly criticizing the all-male-led music industry in interviews. The film's neatly progressive subtext is thus: the men are out of time and out of sync, while the women are modern, with their fingers squarely on the pulse.

Með allt á hreinu remains the most popular film of all time in Iceland, with almost half the nation going to see it on its release. The so-called spring of Icelandic cinema had come into being only two years earlier and the impact of the film in these simpler times can never be overestimated, as social media and its ever-growing content were non-existent then.[22] Quotes from the film found their way into everyday Icelandic language while being simultaneously untranslatable to other languages. As a result, the few foreign audiences that saw it largely left the cinema halls completely dumbfounded. The film and the hullaballoo surrounding it at the time is revelatory in terms of the intense nature of social dynamics in Iceland. Everybody sees a certain film, attends a concert or watches the Eurovision Song Contest. Going back to the 'village' metaphor, it's like when the circus comes to town. Finally, something fun for all of us to do. This situation has lessened somewhat in recent times, in compliance with growing globalization, technological advancements and ever more selective entertainment options. Nonetheless, this metaphor regularly makes itself quite apt.

Stuðmenn established themselves in this decade as the equivalent of Iceland's very own house band, earning the moniker 'Every Icelander's band', a label that still holds. The constant stream of radio hits, successful albums and concerts cemented the status. The creative energy and adventurous spirit the band was enjoying at the time even landed them in China – under the name Strax (Now) – where they played some concerts for unsuspecting but extremely well-behaved crowds. Stuðmenn/Strax were the second band from the Western world to play in such a manner, British pop duo Wham! being the first. Although on quite different terms than either Mezzoforte or The Sugarcubes, this activity nonetheless proved that Icelandic pop music was getting some kind of a foothold on the international scene.

Some vital institutional developments, in terms of the flowering of Icelandic popular music, were put in motion in the 1980s. In a most tumultuous year, 1982, a Battle of the Bands competition had its

A scene from Stuðmenn's legendary film *Með allt á hreinu* (1982), where Akureyri, the capital of the north, serves as the backdrop for some of their musical mischief.

modest beginnings in one of Reykjavík's youth centres, Tónabær (Tone Farm). The competition was initiated by Jóhann G. Jóhannsson, an able and respected musician who had made his mark in the 1960s and '70s, both with Óðmenn and as a solo artist. Jóhann had been bemoaning the lack of opportunities for up-and-coming bands to present their own compositions in a live venue – an annoyance born out of the disco boom – and had met with Tónabær's manager, Ólafur Jónsson, that autumn. The pair decided to do something about this and after some false starts, where established bands played for near-empty rooms, they came up with a new strategy and Músíktilraunir (Music Experiments) was born. By having a few bands with little or no experience playing in a competition, encouraged by friends and well-wishers, at least an audience was guaranteed. In addition, Iceland's most prominent bands played as special guests on the nights, either before the competition or while the audience votes were counted. This exposed the guests to ongoing strands in Icelandic popular music, further enriching the experience. And from that first night on, the competition was a success.

Músíktilraunir would become one of the most important social hubs/greenhouses for young and aspiring pop/rock musicians in the country, a highly valued institution.[23] Its steady run (in operation to this day) and careful management, where the young are nurtured and assisted in their first steps as active musicians, has proven invaluable. Many of Iceland's most high-profile music scenes have been gestated there, for instance Iceland's powerful hip-hop scene at the turn of the millennium. The competition is the only one of its kind that has stuck, and through the decades it has seen the participation, in one way or another, of almost every Icelandic musician who has made their way in the world (the exaggeration here is only slight). Overall, approximately 1,000 bands and artists have entered the competition since its conception.[24]

Icelandic national radio had been established in 1930, and up until 1983 only one channel had been broadcasting. Pop and rock music was rarely heard, save one or two programmes a week. In 1983 Rás 2 (Channel 2) was launched, playing pop and rock music. Three years later, the state monopoly on radio licences was lifted and the first privately owned radio station, Bylgjan (The Wave), was launched. More stations followed, focusing mainly on popular music. In contrast to this, two grassroots stations emerged in 1986 and 1988 respectively and both proved to be influential in the promotion of both Icelandic underground rock and new and exciting music from abroad. One was a college radio station, Útrás; the other, Útvarp Rót, was a wildly independent one with programmers having absolute freedom in their broadcasting criteria.[25] The educational role of these two stations – if unintended – had a deep-rooted cultural effect and they are talked about in a nostalgic, revered tone today.

Bands and artists were quick to consume new fads and fashion strands from abroad in punk's aftermath. Some, like Kukl, opted for grim experimentalism but the synth and New Romantic wave from the UK did not bypass Iceland either. This had been hinted at in the midst of the punk onslaught by the great Bara flokkurinn but a small scene was birthed in 1984–5. Rikshaw were nicknamed 'The Icelandic Duran Duran', not only for their music but for their appearance and overall vibe. Pax Vobis went for the slick, thinking man's pop à la Japan and Sonus Futurae were 'Kraftwerkian'.[26] Most of these bands were short-lived, mustered an album or so each and in the case of Herbert Guðmundsson, a veteran from the 1970s, one mega hit that still lives on, 'Can't Walk Away'. During this period, Grafík, one of Iceland's top pop bands, was also active. Hailing from the Westfjords and led by guitarist Rúnar Þórisson and drummer Rafn Jónsson, it started out as a cold-wave/post-punk-inspired band (although the band had roots in more 'normal' 1970s rock bands), moved on to experimental pastures with complex Zappa-derived instrumentals and then managed to infiltrate the airwaves with engaging New Romantic pop in 1984, now with captivating singer Helgi Björnsson in tow.[27] Quite the ride. The band held on to that position to the end and the final album, *Leyndarmál* (Secret, 1987), featured a new singer, Andrea Gylfadóttir, who was to become one of Iceland's foremost singers in the coming years.[28] There were not many bands going for the earnest U2/Smiths sound-world that was all the rage in the mid-1980s. Rauðir fletir (Red Squares) had a go at it in the years 1986–7 with good results musically but the band was short-lived. Gildran (The Trap) started out with passionate rock in the vein of *War*-era U2, singing heartfelt, meaningful lyrics, and the style was present on their first records in the 1980s.

While The Sugarcubes were sowing the seeds for a proper underground rock scene in Reykjavík, the previously mentioned Músíktilraunir became a breeding ground for pure glossy pop in 1986 when Greifarnir (The Counts), a band from Húsavík – a small town in the north of Iceland – celebrated a landslide victory (a heavy metal band, Gypsy, had won the year before, which says a lot about the wide open policy of the competition).[29] Greifarnir played simple but irresistible pop music, generated for maximum dance floor and hands-in-the-air effects. Their win launched the 'fun-pop' scene that was dominant for the next three years or so and quite influential on later developments in the Icelandic pop scene. The winners in the two subsequent years were of the same ilk and both bands were, like Greifarnir, from the north of the country. Stuðkompaníið (The Jolly Company) from Akureyri, in matching suits and ties, won the 1987 competition and in 1988 the aptly named Jójó (Yo-Yo) – considering the happy-go-lucky oeuvre of the scene – won. The band hailed from Skagaströnd, a small village on the north coast. That year the scene reached its apotheosis, as the bands in second and third place were also a part of this uniquely Icelandic fun-pop brand.

Greifarnir would become one of Iceland's most popular bands in the latter part of the 1980s, quickly releasing two EPs and enjoying a successful run of radio hits and packed-out country dances. They even released an album in 1987, which went against their pure fun image in some respects, containing songs about slavery and child abuse. All of this miraculously went down well with the crowd, the band more or less untouchable by this time.

But let us now go deeper into the workings of Bad Taste (Smekkleysa) and The Sugarcubes, by far the biggest news of the decade in terms of how Icelandic popular music was to develop, both domestically and abroad. Repercussions of the activities born out of these entities cannot be underestimated. Both came into being in 1986, two cornerstones of some musical action in a small island country in the north Atlantic, and the beginning of an international appreciation that the Icelandic pop/rock world still enjoys today. The ideas thrown around in Bad Taste's infancy – some implemented, some not – were to shape the Icelandic avant-garde considerably in the next few years.[30]

'It doesn't matter what you can do, but what you actually do' is a famous quote from Einar Örn and a proclamation from his punk rock days.[31] It's also an apt description for Bad Taste's philosophy, which at the time was a healthy blend of DIY, surrealism and the tried-and-tested Icelandic mantra *þetta reddast*. The label blossomed quickly, albums and books were released in rapid succession and a vibrant underground rock scene immediately formed around The Sugarcubes. Things changed quite dramatically in August 1987, when their song 'Birthday' was released as a single in Britain. The press in the UK went overboard in its praise and when the first album – *Life's Too Good* – was released in 1988 the attention soared even more, both in the UK and the USA.

Bad Taste was given its manifesto in the autumn of 1986, though the actual date of its birth was 8 June the same year. That's when Sindri, the son of Björk and Þór Eldon, was born. Björk and Þór laid the foundation for Bad Taste together with their Sugarcubes band-mates, Einar Örn Benediktsson, Sigtryggur Baldursson, Bragi Ólafsson, Einar Melax and Friðrik Erlingsson.

The Sugarcubes formed in the autumn, like Bad Taste, but the official date of the band's birth is, as in the case of Bad Taste, Sindri's

The Sugarcubes marked a 'year zero' for international interest in Icelandic popular music when their debut album *Life's Too Good* was released in 1988.

birthday. The home of Björk and Þór in downtown Reykjavík was an unofficial centre for all things Bad Taste in the autumn of 1986, many a sleepless night spent formulating progressive ideas on how to be active in Iceland's cultural community. Others who were involved in Bad Taste in the beginning were Ólafur J. Engilbertsson, who had been in the band Fan Houtens kókó along with Þór, the poets Sjón and Jóhamar, and Ásmundur Jónsson and Dóra Jónsdóttir.

The Sugarcubes and Bad Taste followed the same rules in many respects. They both had a unique blend of seriousness, passion and biting, sarcastic humour. Bad Taste was meant to be a general label and publishing house, serving as a platform for the creative ideas of its collective members. Bad Taste is in many ways a very 'Icelandic' thing, especially in the let's-do-it-and-to-hell-with-the-consequences stance. Simple matters of budget are regularly thrown out of the window – a brave, heroic and in some cases even foolhardy philosophy, which at the same time is exactly the reason for the label's success.

Its manifesto bears the boastful title 'World Domination or Death'; a title which describes the infrastructure and idealism of Bad Taste pretty accurately. The manifesto's text is only half-serious and the tone is often sarcastic.[32] The first article references Pablo Picasso's often-quoted assertion that good taste and frugality are the enemies of creativity. Bad Taste's text reads: 'As "good taste" and "financial restraint" are the main enemies of creativity and well-being, Bad Taste will work concertedly against anything that can be categorized as good taste or financial restraint.' This is then further underlined in the next article: '2. In the battle against the above (good taste and so forth), Bad Taste will use all thinkable and unthinkable approaches, such as stuffing things in, tearing them out, tasteless ads and announcements, and distribution and sale of common junk and leftovers.' 'Bad Taste' nights were held – surrealistic happenings where anything and nothing could happen.

The autumn of 1987 saw the first release by The Sugarcubes abroad. 'Birthday' was a single released in the UK by the newly established indie label One Little Indian Records, where the head honcho was The Sugarcubes' old friend Derek Birkett of Flux of Pink Indians 'fame' (in 2020 the name was changed to One Little Independent Records and that name will be used henceforth). The single was chosen as the single of the week by influential music weekly *Melody Maker* and then topped the end-of-the-year Festive Fifty chart on the even more influential John Peel radio show at the BBC ('Oh Fuck!' was Einar Örn's reply when he heard the *Melody Maker* news, a sentence that swiftly made its way into formal meeting minutes of Grammið).[33] The Sugarcubes' debut album *Life's Too Good* was released in 1988 to rave reviews. Quite the impressive debut – fresh and energetic, playfully melodic but arty at the same time.[34] The floodgates were now open and the band became underground darlings, mentioned in the international music press in the same breath as other emerging acts (Pixies, Throwing Muses). For the very first time, an Icelandic act was able to sustain something akin to a career outside of Iceland. The Sugarcubes were no one-hit wonders, or as they proclaimed mockingly themselves: 'The weird thing is that we didn't enter the music business through its rear end . . . we went straight to the top!'[35] The success naturally evoked interest in Iceland as it was quite exotic to the everyman, and even brought sundry visitors to the country (stray tourists at the time were usually met with the quizzical: 'What are you *doing* here?'). The international music press spared no time in writing about Iceland as a fertile ground for music-making, spinning lavish tales about the characteristics of the nation and its perceived connections to the surrounding nature. In this respect, not much has changed: the seeds for the ongoing elves-walking-on-lava stereotypes were sown at this time.

The cynical comment from Þór Eldon at the beginning of this chapter is typical of The Sugarcubes' dealings with the press at the time. But you can also detect a sincere belief: the total freedom to do what bids you, fortified by the notion that no one is listening anyway (as touched upon in the 1970s chapter). This healthy disregard for 'the game', an almost arrogant attitude shaped by naive self-confidence and juvenile ignorance towards what you can and cannot do has been at the heart of many musical export efforts from Iceland in subsequent years, musicians often referencing the devil-may-care work ethic of The Sugarcubes as an inspiration.

The Bad Taste label was now a towering force and tried to use the exposure of The Sugarcubes to advance similarly minded bands from Iceland, all of them on its roster. A compilation album was released internationally in 1990 – of course named *World Domination or Death, Vol. 1* – containing tracks by some of these acts. U.S. tours were set up and distribution deals sealed. The first generation of the so-called 'Bad Taste' bands were either making progress or folding, come the end of the 1980s. Risaeðlan (literal meaning 'Dinosaur' but called Reptile abroad) was one of the main concerns and managed to release an album with some international distribution in 1990: an animated and energetic group, it was led by two vigorous women, Dóra Wonder (Halldóra Geirharðsdóttir), who sang and played the saxophone, and Magga Stína (Margrét Kristín Blöndal), who sang and played the violin. They drew from the same surrealistic well as The Sugarcubes but with a flippant carnival ambience, mixing indie pop strands with world music. The Bad Taste roster was very diverse, HAM were a brutal, gothic noise rock band, influenced by Swans, and One Little Independent released their debut LP in 1989 (*Buffalo Virgin*). HAM would change tactics in the 1990s, inspiring a cult of devotion (more about HAM in the next chapter). Some of the Bad Taste bands were rough-and-ready garage punk rockers, for example Sogblettir (Love Bites) and Bleiku bastarnir (The Pink Raffia Bastards). Langi Seli og Skuggarnir (meaning Long Seal and The Shadows, but calling themselves Oxtor in the international market) played greasy rockabilly, and Bootlegs riffed on straight-up thrash metal. Bad Taste didn't care about genre or style, the character and appeal of the bands was key.

Of course, interesting underground bands were not necessarily signed to Bad Taste. Rosebud was a young, Velvet Underground-inspired indie rock group with all the right moves and it's a crying shame that an album never saw the light of day. Daisy Hill Puppy Farm featured a young Jóhann Jóhannsson. S.H. Draumur (Black and White Dream) delivered highly melodic underground rock infused with excellent Icelandic lyrics (recalling the socio-realistic genius of Spilverk þjóðanna at times). The band reached its apex on the masterpiece *Goð* (1987). The band then became Bless and found shelter among the Bad Taste groups.

On the other end of the spectrum, a pure pop movement was taking hold domestically, with driven bands filling the airwaves as

Sálin hans Jóns míns remain one of Iceland's biggest pop bands. This photo was taken in 1991, when the band was at the height of its powers.

well as the dance halls in the rural areas with music and philosophies that could not have been further from the underground activities. This 'movement' had confidence and the music was ambitious, taking its cue in part from the blue-eyed sophisti-pop that was coming from the USA and the UK in the late 1980s. The main bands were Sálin hans Jóns míns (The Soul of My John), Nýdönsk (New Danish), Todmobile and Síðan skein sól (And Then the Sun Broke Through). The peculiar band names are in stark contrast to the catchy pop that was on their records.[36] Sálin hans Jóns míns played soul-infused music at first, before going for melodic pop and rock that's hard to describe for a non-Icelander (the band became huge and still has a fervent following). Nýdönsk played intelligent, accomplished pop and had an astounding run with their first four albums, released from 1989 to 1992 – excellent works one and all. Todmobile offered epic, neo-classical pop while Síðan skein sól adopted a more rock-oriented, new wave-lite direction at the beginning before streamlining their approach. Their singer, Helgi Björnsson (Helgi Björns, of Grafík fame), was a drama school-educated charisma bomb and had a cool rocking swagger not unlike Pétur Kristjánsson and Rúnar Júlíusson before him. He has managed to utilize this persona throughout his career and is one of Iceland's best-known pop icons today.[37] Stjórnin (The Board) were also huge at the end of the 1980s/start of the 1990s and were blatantly pop – no extra frills, sarcasm or cleverness, just pure, unadulterated pop for the masses, who swallowed all of it whole.

The 1990s would then see the fruition of various scenes, especially in the underground, where Iceland was following international developments quite closely in stark contrast with the belated arrival of punk.

Björk stands out as a unique figure in Icelandic music, recognized as the most celebrated Icelander in history.

5

The 1990s: The World Domination of Björk

The Sugarcubes split in December 1992 after three albums: one brilliant LP, followed by a somewhat underwhelming album (*Here Today, Tomorrow Next Week!*, 1989) and then a final effort that served as a commendable parting shot (*Stick Around for Joy*, 1992). Björk would launch her solo career six months later with radical consequences for the Icelandic pop/rock scene, pushing Iceland into the international limelight and contributing in no small means to its overall visibility, playing a part in the tourist boom that the country is enjoying (or enduring) at the time of writing. Björk is now the most famous Icelander who has ever lived, usually the first thing people mention when Iceland comes up in a discussion.

Björk's first international album, simply called *Debut*, was released in June 1993, on One Little Independent (we discount her effort from 1977, detailed in the 1970s chapter; *Gling-Gló* doesn't count either, an LP she did with a jazz trio in 1990, covering a selection from the Icelandic songbook –a stellar album it must be said, and a big seller still for Bad Taste). The first single, 'Human Behaviour', entered the UK Top 40, accompanied by a quirky video made by in-vogue director Michel Gondry. Björk would go from strength to strength, releasing two more hugely successful albums in this decade – *Post* in 1995 and *Homogenic* in 1997 – solidifying her unique vision with every release. She became a critics' darling, regularly topping end-of-year lists, gathering all kinds of accolades while a legion of fans, bordering on the cult-like, was formed. Timing played a significant role in Björk's immense popularity. After Nirvana upended the mainstream in 1991, major labels were flooded with avant-garde-leaning artists and the heavy airplay of Beck's solidly weird 'Loser' in 1994 seemed to crystallize this state of affairs. Björk's world slotted in perfectly.

Back home, fertile scenes sprang up, mirroring similar genre developments internationally. Iceland mustered a kind of micro-edition of foreign scenes, constricted, of course, by its small population. For instance, quite active death metal, indie rock and grunge scenes were cultivated – burning bright, but only for a short span of time. Electronica and experimental music also thrived in the underground and seeds for a future hip-hop scene were sown mid-decade, led by the rap-rock hybrid band Quarashi and Subterranean, a more straightforward hip-hop crew (and at the same time, a multicultural one, a rarity in Iceland). All of these scenes used both Icelandic and English in their lyrics and all of them were supported by Músíktilraunir, which emerged as an established cultural entity in this decade, an important fertilizer for the grassroot, whatever the crop was at any given time.

Sororicide, who would become the undisputed kings of death metal, took shape in early 1990. The band went on to win Músíktilraunir in 1991, a good example of the competition's ability to reflect the latest strands in Iceland's garages.[1] The members were mere teenagers – between fifteen and seventeen – considering that their counterparts in the USA and Sweden, the cradles of the first wave of death metal, tended to be a few years older. Despite this, Sororicide were extremely skilled as a band, comparable to any of the foreign bands in the international death metal scene.[2] In hindsight, it's unfortunate that possibilities for proper export and exposure were very limited at the time, although the band became known in collectors' tape trading circles. A full-blown death metal movement unfolded a year later, the Músíktilraunir competition being its main platform, and in 1992 the jury enjoyed (or endured) long nights of punishing death metal from varyingly competent bands (yes, I was there). Only three bands – and also the best of the lot – mustered releases. Along with Sororicide (who released an album, *The Entity*, on LP/CD in 1991) the terrifying Cranium released their work *Abduction* on cassette (1993), which contained highly aggressive and almost blackened death metal brew, and Strigaskór nr. 42 (Sneakers no. 42) released *Blót* on CD in 1994, a progressive death metal album that's simply astonishing, blending melodies from Icelandic folk songs into a quite unique take on the death metal form. The year 1994 was also when Icelandic death metal evaporated rather swiftly from the noise-infested garages. We also have to mention grindcore legends Forgarður helvítis (Courtyard of Hell), who formed in 1991 in the south by two sets of cousins from farms near the open ocean. It's the most brutal music ever committed to tape in Icelandic music history, as can be heard on their cassette release *Brennið kirkjur* (Burn Churches, 1995) and the CD *Gerningaveður* (2002).[3]

Generally speaking, Icelandic heavy metal has a rather interesting history, mostly because it was almost non-existent for an unusually long period of time (quite contrary to the high visibility and activity it enjoys today, putting Iceland firmly alongside other heavy metal loving Nordic countries). Some single out Icecross's eponymous debut from 1973 as the first Icelandic heavy metal album, a reputation born mainly out of its strikingly dark cover (it looks like some raw proto-black metal album from the 1980s) and the grim and quite heavy blues-rock within (it's quite the stretch to call it heavy metal though). Start was a band formed in the early 1980s by 1970s rock veteran Pétur Kristjánsson; they had the look (and fonts!) but the music itself only hinted at metal. It's not until 1983 that a true heavy metal band steps up. Drýsill (Gnome, or Devil) managed an album in 1985, containing a rocking NWOBHM-inspired heavy metal (New Wave Of British Heavy Metal). It was led by the red-haired Viking Eiríkur Hauksson, a singer/musician who would go on to become a fixture in Icelandic music culture at large. He is a versatile musician, competing in Eurovision with pop acts and singing with Norwegian thrashers ARTCH without blinking an eye, enjoying full respect from both camps while he was at it.[4] Around that time, bands like Gypsy, Þrumuvagninn (Chariot of Thunder) and later Exizt came along and the music got even heavier at the tail end of the 1980s, with bands like Túrbó and Bootlegs playing thrash metal. But there was no scene yet, still just stray bands doing their thing.[5]

The death metal scene was the first real heavy metal scene, seeing dozens of bands and lasting a few years. There were several reasons that made it possible to prosper. First, the band members were all teenagers and concerts were often held in Reykjavík's various youth centres and colleges, and at city council-organized festivals. The 'village' factor directing the Icelandic music industry and the proximity within it played its natural part as well. Friendships were forged between like-minded individuals; tapes were traded and the few import death metal albums were passed around. The bands hailed from different neighbourhoods in the capital area, and various meeting points, like the concerts mentioned, were utilized to their fullest. These gatherings allowed people to connect, form bands and nurture the scene's lifeblood.

Grunge established itself in Iceland but did not run parallel to developments in the USA, unlike the death metal scene. The leading names here were active when the second wave (sometimes called post-grunge) was taking hold in the USA (*c.* 1993–6), yet playing music mostly inspired by the first wave, with an emphasis on the slick metal-derived grunge of Alice in Chains, Soundgarden and, up to a point, Pearl Jam, rather than the raw fuzz of Mudhoney and early Nirvana.[6] Names include Dos Pilas, Bone China, Quicksand Jesus, Dead Sea Apple and In Bloom. The last even made a foray into Los Angeles and tried to 'make it'. Other bands worth mentioning, mining '90s hard rock if not straight-up grunge, were Lipstick Lovers, Stripshow and the oh-so-heavy Bleeding Volcano. Hallur Ingólfsson, Bleeding

Volcano's leader (and formerly of Gypsy and HAM), then went on to form XIII in 1993, releasing great albums with cold European gothic and industrial influences that put them in a quite unique place, at least domestically (the albums pricked some ears overseas as well).

One band managed to get in sync with and ride the first wave of grunge. In a way. The amusingly named Deep Jimi and the Zep Creams were road-hardened youngsters from Keflavík who simply flew to New York in the same month that Nirvana released *Nevermind* (September 1991) and tried their luck. The Atlantic label, scurrying for anything resembling Nirvana in the immediate aftermath, released an album, *Funky Dinosaur*, in 1992. It promptly sank without a trace but Icelanders followed the news with glee.

The most popular 'traditional' rock band of this decade was Jet Black Joe and their self-titled debut album from 1992 was an absolute monster hit.[7] The music was hard rock with heavy emphasis on classic rock from the late 1960s and 1970s. Members wore hippy garb, projected a Zeppelin-like ambiance and even threw in some flute playing. The band was tight, and main songwriter Gunnar Bjarni had a touch of Noel Gallagher about him, writing songs that reminded people of timeless rock anthems. The main asset was Páll Rózinkranz's golden voice, a marvellously controlled baritone that soared to all the necessary heights when needed. More albums followed, the usual efforts to export were tried, but the band ran its course shortly after the mid-1990s.

Before we leave the town of rock 'n' roll it's necessary to assess HAM – the gothic noise rockers we touched upon in the preceding chapter – and their importance to Icelandic rock culture, which has proved to be pivotal. The band began to streamline their sound at the beginning of the 1990s (but only just), spewing out blackly humorous but at the same time epic and crushing rock and roll. A fanatic following in the underground circles began to take shape: HAM's concerts were now like a mass for the converted who mouthed every lyric, hailing the band as demigods. When the band played their farewell show in 1994 their legendary status was secured and their subsequent activity since the year 2001, with sporadic album releases and live concerts, has edged them towards something that could be called mainstream acceptance. The band's cult status is hard to explain to non-Icelanders, and curious music fans from abroad have sometimes been flabbergasted by the popularity and the sacred aura that surrounds the band that plays 'gothic heavy metal with a comic twist', as Björk once said. Something is inevitably lost in translation, a certain domestic appeal which can only be fully appreciated and understood by being born and raised here.

The pure pop movement, which gained a foothold at the end of the 1980s, was the foremost mainstream concern at the start of the 1990s and would remain intact throughout the decade. These bands had no real ambitions to make it abroad, instead playing at country dances and aiming to be playlisted on Icelandic daytime radio. They were (and are) strictly a domestic concern, unknown to foreigners seeking bands from the 'hip' scene of Reykjavík. At the same time the bands were, interestingly enough, prone to artistic ambitions as described in the 1980s chapter, thus running a twofold career, on the one hand playing lighter material on a Saturday night but on the other releasing studio albums with serious, thinking person's pop music. Sálin hans Jóns míns even released two linked concept albums at the start of the 2000s, eventually turning them into a musical. A second wave of these bands would occur at the start of the 2000s.

Parallel to the death metal rumblings, a strong indie/alt-rock scene started to blossom. It was kickstarted in 1992 by Kolrassa krókríðandi (later Bellatrix), an all-girl unit that played indie rock with a nod to the ongoing UK shoegaze scene (Ride, Lush, My Bloody Valentine and others).[8] Kolrassa's win at Músíktilraunir that year signified a new 'spring' in Icelandic indie that was felt deeply in the years to come. In fact, this spring was a generational change – the old Bad Taste/Sugarcubes vanguard that had been very prominent in the late 1980s made way for younger players who were strongly influenced by those very musicians. The mantle was thus passed on gracefully and it was fitting that the Bad Taste label released Kolrassa's first record, a mini-LP called *Drápa* (Poem) that Christmas. From the beginning, Kolrassa – as it's sometimes abbreviated – were one of the scene's leading lights and in the following years, many note-worthy bands that would emerge in the scene took their first steps through Músíktilraunir. Maus entered the competition fully formed in 1994 and won it, drawing influences from Icelandic post-punk, 1980s gothic-tinged pop à la The Cure and even Duran Duran, while delivering a unique sound, dynamic yet melodic, with riveting live performances to match.[9] Their albums would deliver on all these promises. The indie rock scene was in full swing in 1995 when a band from 'rock town' Hafnarfjörður won with simple but attention-grabbing, grunge-influenced rock. Botnleðja (Silt) were menacing – more Melvins than Pearl Jam – but still, the music was intrinsically catchy and soon enough Botnleðja would be the reigning kings of Icelandic alternative rock. Songs by Maus, Botnleðja, Kolrassa and affiliated bands started to creep onto the radio, the scene enjoying a minor mainstream success for a while. Other bands worth mentioning are Stjörnukisi (Star Kitten) fronted by the inimitable Úlfur Chaka Karlsson, playing captivating alt-rock influenced by harsh American underground rock (The Jesus Lizard, Slint), and Ensími, a band built around veterans from the death metal scene and including two members from the defunct Jet Black Joe. Their two albums at the end of the 1990s were perfectly realized, sturdy alt-rock albums, the latter partly produced by legendary American noisenik producer Steve Albini. Yukatan, who had won Músíktilraunir in 1993, came on like a polyrhythmic Primus, with wunderkind Ólafur Björn Ólafsson (Óbó) behind the kit. Lastly, 200,000 naglbítar (200,000 Pincers) was a sprightly, harmonizing indie rock band from Akureyri. Fronted by two brothers, their three albums (from 1998 to 2003) are genuine classics from that fruitful, all-Icelandic indie rock era.

Alongside the 'visible' underground scenes were scenes that were more buried: all kinds of noisy punk rock bands and experimental groups whose music was to be found on cassette compilations and self-released albums. The F.I.R.E. group was one of the more active art-collectives of that kind in the mid-1990s, releasing a CD compilation, organizing gigs and bringing in foreign underground bands. Four bands founded F.I.R.E. and their different styles say a lot about how inclusive the small underground scene in Iceland was (and needed to be) at this time. Stilluppsteypa were noise experimentalists, one-man band Curver delved into feedback-drenched underground rock à la Spacemen 3 and Loop, and Púff played hard-to-define, avant-rock. The fourth band was Kolrassa krókríðandi.

The proximity of the indie and experimental scenes connected people where the only commonality was a strong interest in music from off the beaten tracks, whatever the type. The cementing of friendships and musical activities followed the same trajectory as the death metal bands and given the underground factor of both scenes, there was also a 'hang out' overlap, death metal dudes going out with indie girls and so on. And of course, many bands that were active in these productive times never managed to preserve their music in physical form, playing a few gigs for some months and then disappearing.[10] The concert bills around this time were quite inclusive, featuring a variety of bands from different scenes playing together on the same night. This demonstrated that there's limited room for specialization in a society that supports active yet small music scenes. 'Village' living for a rock fan means that you have to make do with what's available on any given night. For instance, when a home-grown grunge band performed, the crowd would reflect a diverse spectrum, including death metallers, hard rockers, pop rockers and more.

The decade was somewhat characterized by possibilities that had always been out of reach. Björk had swung the gates open and the art-collective GusGus was the first Icelandic group to fully capitalize on it. The foreign media was on the prowl, looking for eccentric, cool music from Iceland and GusGus ticked all the 'hipper than thou' boxes: a group of directors, musicians, fashion designers, photographers and others from the downtown 101 Reykjavík area – nine in all – as talented and experienced as they were undeniably cool. The members already had some international connections and balanced arty heft and business savvy with ease. The band signed a contract with respected British independent label 4AD in the summer of 1996 and a year later their international debut album, *Polydistortion*, was released, containing a blend of minimal techno and soul-infused electro-pop.[11] The media coverage GusGus enjoyed was a good indication of what was to come – that is, meanderings about elves, quirkiness, lava and volcanos. The band did little to fend it off and happily partook in photo shoots amid snowy mountain backdrops. The attitude towards this among Icelandic musicians is mixed, as will be apparent, some using the hyperbole to their advantage while others shun it.

The GusGus collective stepped confidently through the doors opened up by Björk in the 1990s and fortified the idea of Iceland and Reykjavík as a hip and cool place, music-wise.

Around the mid-1990s, more artists grabbed these new-found opportunities with both hands and tried their luck at 'making it'. Unun (Enjoyment) was an indie rock group, led by one Dr. Gunni, a veteran from the 1980s underground scene (S.H. Draumur) and an esteemed pop historian as well, often referenced in this book. The band also featured Þór Eldon, The Sugarcubes' former guitarist, and the charismatic songstress Heiða Eiríksdóttir. The band released an album internationally in 1995 (*Super Shiny Dreams*) and jumped wholeheartedly through fame's merciless wringer. The music was good, the band tight and the efforts proper but returns were diminishing. Bang Gang experimented with the boy/girl set-up, the stern look of the mastermind, Barði Jóhannsson, balancing the diva looks of singer Esther Talía Casey and the music a sort of tundra version of Yazoo, melodic electronica reflecting the downtempo/trip hop fashion of the day. The duo released an album domestically in 1998 (*You*) and then signed to East West France, which released the album internationally in 2000. Bang Gang, which is in reality the solo project of Barði, has managed to keep an international presence since. Another band ploughing a similar furrow was Lhooq. Jóhann Jóhannsson, the future post-classical and soundtrack composer extraordinaire, and Pétur Hallgrímsson, a guitar whizz who has worked with Kylie Minogue, Sigur Rós and John Grant, made up the group, both veterans from the 1980s underground scene. Along with singer Sara Marti, they produced haunting trip-hop-inspired pop, drawing from Massive Attack and Portishead. The results were released on an eponymous album in 1998 through the British label Echo but the band was short-lived and success only moderate. Emilíana Torrini is a singer and musician who first made an impact in Iceland with two albums of cover versions released in 1995 and 1996. An album was released internationally through One Little Independent in 1999 (*Love in the Time of Science*), launching an international career. We will take a closer look at Emilíana in the next chapter.

The last name that we need to put under the microscope in all of those mid-1990s fame try-outs is Bellatrix, which was the international name for Kolrassa krókríðandi. Mainstreaming their sound, they went full-on indie pop in 1998 and made a respectable stab at pop stardom around the millennium. Relocating to London, no time was spared in working the business, playing concerts and touring (a joint headlining tour with Coldplay in 2000 for instance). The band signed with indie label Fierce Panda, which released the album *It's All True* in 2000. A single, 'Jediwannabe', peaked at number 65 in the UK singles chart in September but the band broke up a little under a year after.

From the mid- to late 1990s, ever more artists took similar steps towards the international stage. They varied in type – the more resilient indie bands tried their hand at English lyrics, a more 'appropriate' image and even a name change. Contemporary fads such as trip hop were tested out and a foreseeable dose of arty, Nordic ice princesses à la Björk also emerged. The advent of the Internet also made it possible for fringe musicians to distribute their material to remote regions, a development that began at a grassroots level before it reached mainstream areas.

A good example of this was the electronica/techno label Thule, founded in 1995, which released Icelandic techno artists domestically and abroad through tightly integrated networks that spread throughout the ever-expanding Internet-based music world. In harmony with the futuristic elements of the music itself, Icelandic techno pioneers were quick to adapt to technological developments. Thule also confirmed that a healthy electronica/techno/house scene had been thriving and developing in Iceland, in sync with foreign scenes. Hardcore and rave acts, such as Ajax, had been established early in the decade and warehouse raves were held. Ajax comprised Þórhallur Skúlason, aka Thor, the 'Godfather of Icelandic techno', and Sigurbjörn 'Biogen' Þorgrímsson, who would go on to become a legendary and influential figure in Icelandic electronic music.[12] The Icelandic techno/house community was active but mostly underground and its workings were evident in artists like Björk, who infused her albums with electronic elements, as well as the previously mentioned GusGus, which had members straight from that scene. Acts birthed by Thule included Exos, Cold and Ozy (initially Ozzy), most of them going for cold, dub-infused minimal techno. The Icelandic dance culture had many facets in the 1990s, such as radio shows, club nights and concerts, and the infamous Uxi festival in 1995 revolved mostly around that kind of music.[13] A baggy-inspired, Madchester-oriented band, Bubbleflies, also ruffled some feathers (Thor being one of the founders), marrying rock and dance/electronica on their debut album, *The World Is Still Alive* (1993).

Scenes that had been long established internationally came to prominence in Iceland in the 1990s, such as experimental music of the 'outer limits' kind. In the 1970s and '80s this subculture had been almost non-existent. In *Rokk í Reykjavík*, Bruni BB, a notorious performance group, was shown in full action where hens were slaughtered, along with some music. That was pretty much the full extent of mainstream exposure of that kind of music-making at the time, if we can call a documentary on punk rock mainstream. Other artists were deeply entrenched in the underground and while performances were made, releases were impossibly scarce.

Cassette compilations began to appear more frequently at the end of the 1980s and start of the 1990s. Alongside various types of underground rock you sometimes found deeply experimental works, atonal and unforgiving, commonly tucked away at the end of the tape. Bad Taste, then the reigning avant-garde label, fostered some of the artists but most of them released their stuff independently when it came to putting out free-standing albums and works. Inferno 5 and Graupan are fine early 1990s examples of this, but the biggest news relates to two bands, Reptilicus and Stilluppsteypa, both of them managing to impact the international experimental music markets.

Reptilicus released a cassette in 1990, *Temperature of Blood*, influenced by 1980s industrial acts like Throbbing Gristle, Skinny Puppy and the early material of Front 242 and Einstürzende Neubauten. In the early 1990s the band started to gain traction in the international industrial/avant-garde scene, mainly through their contact with the UK-based World Serpent Distribution (Current 93, Coil, Nurse with Wound). Stilluppsteypa started out as an anarcho-punk band in the Crass vein but quickly delved into noise/sound art and would go on to release quite the quantity of such music internationally, on many labels and on many formats. Both Reptilicus and Stilluppsteypa garnered attention in the global experimental music scene, a realm fuelled by passionate tape trading and letter writing, a music fan culture amplified nowadays by the Internet, which has enabled fans and bands themselves to share connections and forge new opportunities for reaching audiences.

An important collective was set up at the tail end of the 1990s, in summer 1999 to be exact. Kitchen Motors (Tilraunaeldhúsið in Icelandic, 'The Experimental Kitchen') was born out of club evenings and concerts where musicians from different scenes and generations worked together.[14] The collective was led by Kristín Björk Kristjánsdóttir aka Kira Kira, an underground musician, Hilmar Jensson, one of Iceland's best-known experimental jazz guitarists, and Jóhann Jóhannsson.[15] Some years into the 2000s Kitchen Motors released CDs and organized gigs, exhibitions, performances and the like, slowly advancing as a formidable force in the Icelandic underground. Apparat Organ Quartet, of which Jóhann was a member, was originally conceived as a collaborative project for a concert series curated by Kitchen Motors. The Quartet, effectively a quintet (the 'biggest quartet in the world!' as one member proclaimed), made quite the impression at the start of the decade, its riff-driven, Kraftwerkian organ orgy, topped with motorik Krautrock beats, making quite the spectacle.[16] We'll look closer at Jóhann's career in the next chapter.

In 1999 Árni Matthíasson, Iceland's most prominent music writer at the time, wrote an article in which he gathered information on Icelandic pop/rock artists chasing the dream of industry success, referencing fellow journalists from abroad who had been following the Icelandic scene and its export possibilities.[17] Some of the key characteristics that the outside ears heard in Icelandic pop were self-deprecating and surreal humour, a DIY mentality and a kind of wide-eyed disregard for unspoken but well-established rules concerning behaviour in the pop/rock world (discussed earlier in relation to The Sugarcubes). They also mentioned that each and every band seemed to represent a genre of their own. This sentiment was reiterated some years later by Nick Prior, who found that 'Reykjavík's compact spatial configuration is a key condition for these internal logics of division,' referencing that the proximity of the bands gives way to a need for differentiation, rather than contributing to sameness. Reykjavík musicians, interviewed by Prior, confirmed the need to sound different from friends who were practising next door.[18] Árni also noted in his article that active bands soon found a need to play abroad as the home market was so small, highlighting statements already made about that reality. The highest-selling vinyl records in the 1980s, for instance, shifted 30,000 copies, which represented massive sales in Iceland but not enough to sustain a living. Internet advancements in the 1990s soon made it easier to establish connections abroad and, together with the rising interest in all things Icelandic, bands moved on to the international stage in higher numbers than ever before. For the first time, they started to achieve something more than fifteen minutes of fame.

The band Sigur Rós had been formed on New Year's Eve, 1994, in a small town northeast of Reykjavík (Mosfellsbær). First called Victory Rose (a direct translation of the Icelandic name) they soon switched to the Icelandic version (the band was named after singer/guitarist Jón Þór Birgisson (Jónsi)'s youngest sister, Sigurrós, born in late 1993). The band was a trio in the beginning: besides Jónsi the group included Georg Holm on bass and Ágúst Ævar Gunnarsson on drums. A hippyish bunch, drawing on recent shoegaze and grunge trends, they quickly established themselves as a popular live draw in the Reykjavík underground scene and in 1997 their first album, *Von* (Hope), was released on Bad Taste Records. *Von* is a muddled and long-winded ambient-laden affair, not quite capturing the epic music of the band's live shows.[19] In 1999 their second album, *Ágætis byrjun* (A Nice Start), was released. Kjartan Sveinsson, on keyboards and various instruments, had joined the band by this time. Ási, the head of Bad Taste, was hoping to sell about 1,500–2,000 copies but instead the album became a phenomenal success, both in its native country and abroad.[20] Entrenched in the post-rock landscape of the time and undeniably beautiful, the album was critically lauded and became a cult hit, the music compared to 'god weeping tears of gold in heaven'.[21] The album has sold several million copies today and the band has worldwide success comparable only to Björk. We will delve deeper into the Sigur Rós journey in the 2000s chapter, a period when their career began to soar.

In 1999 the first Iceland Airwaves music festival was held, a yearly festival in Reykjavík that has proved to be one of the more substantial cultural institutions with regard to the Icelandic pop/rock world.[22] It welcomes both Icelandic and international artists and is, along with Músíktilraunir, the single most important event in the country's music calendar.[23] The Icelandic bands put on their 'good clothes', knowing that label sharks are potentially in the crowd. It's akin to an annual festival for the industry at large, a platform for ideas exchange and real-world meet-ups for people connected solely by email for most of the year. Coincidentally, it was Sigur Rós's concert at the Reykjavík Free Church at that festival, in the autumn of 2000, that ignited a bidding war between the big international record labels, leading to MCA releasing the band's album *( )* ('The Bracket Album') in 2002 and with that, skyrocketing the band to pastures unknown, as much as you can skyrocket a staunch underground band.

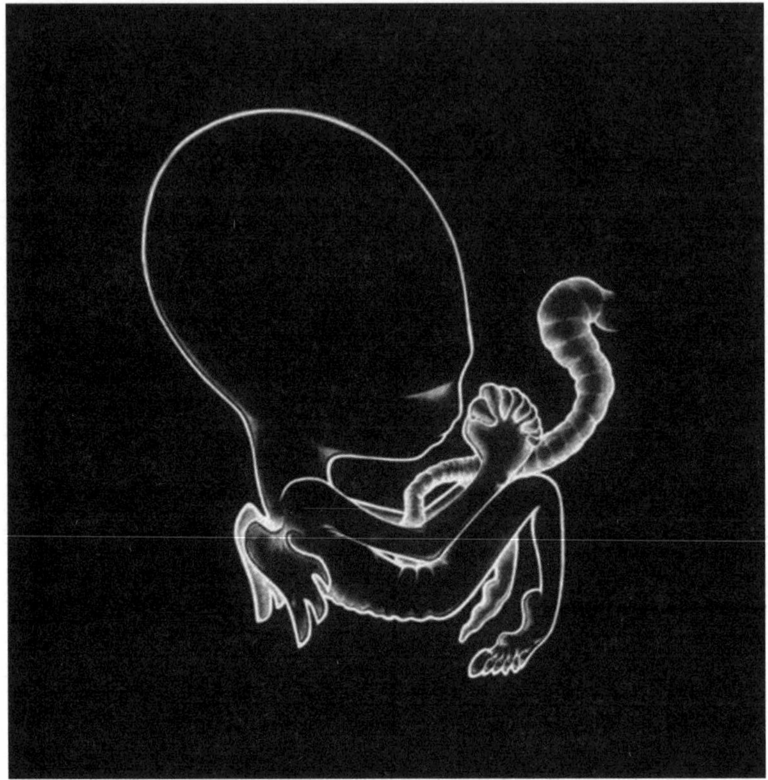

Sigur Rós's second album *Ágætis byrjun* (1999) made them international stars, second only to Björk in terms of gravitas and respect.

More institutional changes occurred in the 1990s. X-ið (The X) was an alt-rock radio station that played underground and left-field music 24/7, drastically influencing the youth of that era. It was the only station of its kind at the time and continues to operate today, its initial rise a part of the broader popularity of alternative music during the grunge/Nirvana revolution.

Record store culture is often a key driver in fostering music scenes (see Rough Trade in the UK, for example). In the 1980s and '90s there were a few stores of various types in Reykjavík: major label stores, independent ones (with an underground emphasis) and stray second-hand ones, albeit that sector was very underdeveloped at the time. Grammið was the most important underground outlet in the 1980s and the opening of Hljómalind in 1991 was a crucial addition to that field. The store imported talked-about underground records, supported the emerging dance/electronic scene and served as a communal gathering place. The charismatic 1980s scenester Kiddi Kanína ran the store. Nearing the decade's end, the almighty 12 Tónar store opened and the second-hand business finally started to shape up.

In the 1990s, as in previous decades, local heroes emerged – musicians who became extremely popular in Iceland but had little impact beyond its borders. The key to their success was their ability to appeal to different generations and diverse tastes. KK, Kristján Kristjánsson, was a busker playing blues in Scandinavia before moving back to Iceland at the start of the 1990s. He released his debut album in 1991, at the tender age of 35, and the album, titled *Lucky One*, became a big success. He followed it up with the superb *Bein leið* (Straight Ahead) the year after. KK's easy charm, roots in the blues, and delightfully simple, first-rate melodies won him radio play and numerous gigs. While mainstream success beckoned, he retained a gritty rock 'n' roll edge that underground-minded listeners found hard to resist. His career flourished in the 1990s, each and every release a success. He achieved this with his band (KK Band), as a solo artist and in collaboration with Magnús Eiríksson of Mannakorn.

Another example of this, but highly different musically, is Páll Óskar (Paul Oscar), *the* pop star of Iceland and an important gay icon. Like KK, Páll Óskar came into his own at the start of the 1990s, participating in a hugely successful stage production of the *Rocky Horror Show* where he played the lead, Frank-N-Furter, at twenty years of age. After that, the decade belonged to him, where he displayed a remarkable range of musical styles, quickly becoming Iceland's best-loved pop star, a position he has held onto to this day. His debut album, *Stuð* (1993), was produced by Jóhann Jóhannsson and Sigurjón Kjartansson of HAM, underpinning Páll Óskar's 'ears-to-the-ground' credentials. An unabashed tribute to disco with postmodern, sarcastic wit (the songs bore names like (translated) 'Endless Joviality', 'Party Animal' and the like). His subsequent LPs were varied; he made a Latin/bossa nova/mambo album with the band Milljónamæringarnir (The Millionaires), a crooner album, a rave album and a big band album, and ended the decade with a full-on nuevo electro/dance album with probably the most tongue-in-cheek title ever, *Deep Inside Paul Oscar*. Let's not forget his groundbreaking Eurovision performance in 1996, where he pushed everything to the limit, musically and performance-wise. Getting a popped-up version of a fourteenth-century French madrigal on to daytime radio was also quite the feat.

As the decade drew to a close, a few mini-revolutions were on the horizon, encompassing hardcore, hip-hop and a revival in the all-Icelandic pop music scene.

6

The 2000s: Sigur Rós and the Icelandic Popular Music Phenomenon

> Church. Reverence. Candles. And profound silence. There is no mistaking it – the band Sigur Rós is about to give a concert. And the people gathered are visibly holding their breath in anticipation . . . All the songs played this evening, except for two, have not yet been released and they are quite different from the songs found on *Ágætis byrjun*. Delicately crafted yet stripped to their essence, these melodies seem to delve deeper into emotion and atmosphere than structured form . . . Many of them sounded, at the time they were performed, like the most beautiful song in the world. A song that I intend to call 'The organ song', as song titles are not yet available, possesses a truly incredible organ interlude, a part that elevates listeners to celestial heights . . . Describing a Sigur Rós concert involves a great deal of dramatic adjectives, and often it is difficult to justify such intensity to oneself. Not this time.

This is an excerpt from a review I wrote for *Morgunblaðið* in the autumn of 2000, after Sigur Rós had played at the Reykjavík Free Church in Reykjavík as part of the Iceland Airwaves festival. The festival was having its first real year of operation after having a trial run of sorts the year before, in a hangar at the Reykjavík airport. The review was justly titled 'Hour of Peace'.[1]

After the release concert of *Ágætis byrjun* in June 1999, founding member Ágúst Ævar Gunnarsson left Sigur Rós. In his place came Orri Páll Dýrason. A pivotal moment in the band's history then came in the autumn of 2000 with that magnificent church concert. In 1999 the string quartet amiina also began collaborating with the band, providing strings for Sigur Rós's music during tours and studio recordings in the subsequent years.[2]

After the church concert, it became evident that Sigur Rós were decidedly uninterested in conforming to mainstream trends with their art. The record deal that was struck with MCA had various conditions, some of which were obscure, highlighting that artistry took precedence over commercial interests.

This whirlwind of attention did not deter the band from continuing with what was the foundation of it all, the music. They began to establish their own studio at the old swimming pool in Álafosskvos in Mosfellsbær, a studio that notably became known as Sundlaugin (The Pool, still in operation). Work on *( )* ('The Bracket Album') began in early 2001 (containing some of the tracks from the church concert). Progress on the album was slow, as the band was constantly on the move. By mid-year, Sigur Rós were generating some buzz abroad, with stars like Lars Ulrich of Metallica and Tommy Lee of Mötley Crüe expressing their admiration. In December a film by Cameron Crowe, *Vanilla Sky*, was premiered, featuring Sigur Rós songs, including 'Untitled 4', known as 'Njósnavélin' (The Spy Machine; also known as 'The Nothing Song'), which was yet to be released.[3]

The band's side projects were numerous in 2002. In April, for example, 'Hrafnagaldur Óðins' was performed at the Reykjavík Arts Festival, a collaboration with Hilmar Örn Hilmarsson (HÖH), Steindór Andersen and others. 'The Bracket Album' finally saw the light of day in the autumn, with its stark presentation clearly intended to let the music speak for itself, along with the fact that there were no lyrics. Jónsi sang in Vonlenska (Hopelandic), a 'language' built on made-up words that resemble the phonology of the Icelandic language. The album was more meticulous and darker than *Ágætis byrjun*, with its eight tracks divided into two sections and with a 36-second silence at the album's midpoint.[4]

Three years passed between the intricate and meticulous ( ) and *Takk...*, where the band ventured into a different realm, even popping things up a bit, but without losing the characteristics and qualities that had made them the most famous rock band to have ever graced the country. Members had been busy with various projects in the meantime, Jónsi had emerged as Frakkur and Kjartan had appeared as The Lonesome Traveller along with Orri and amiina's violinist María Huld Markan Sigfúsdóttir (Kjartan and María were now a married couple). The band's music for the documentary *Hlemmur* was released in 2003 on the band's own Krúnk label in limited quantity and sold on their European and American tours that spring. That same year the band composed music for the choreographer Merce Cunningham, which he used in his work *Split Sides* (the music was released in 2004 as the EP 'Ba Ba Ti Ki Di Do').

The album-making process for *Takk...* took twenty months, a somewhat traditional time frame for Sigur Rós. The recordings for ( ) had been challenging, and there was a deliberate effort to spice things up a bit. The band was now under EMI in the UK and Geffen in the USA, both renowned and stable companies. Sigur Rós had become big, with substantial activity, and their manager, John Best, spent a great deal of time sifting through endless collaboration offers from various quarters.

A single, 'Glósóli' ('Sæglópur' in the USA), was released approximately a month before the album. 'Hoppípolla' was then released in November and was set to make an impact. In fact, the members jokingly called it 'The Money Song', suspecting it would do well commercially. And it did, reaching number 24 on the UK charts in May 2006, marking the band's highest chart placement to date. The song had been featured on the BBC series *Planet Earth* and that

The breathtaking beauty of Sigur Rós's music earned them universal acclaim in the 2000s.

contributed to its popularity. The song was used in numerous films, TV shows and even at football stadiums to pump up the crowd. The techno artist Chicane took the song into the UK top ten with a version he called 'Poppiholla', and the American indie rock band We Are Scientists covered it as well. 'Sæglópur' was then re-released as a four-track EP in the summer of 2006, including three previously unreleased songs.

In the summer of 2005 Sigur Rós embarked on their most extensive tour to date. On Sunday, 27 November that year, the band performed in Laugardalshöll, marking their first domestic concert in three years. There was great anticipation surrounding the concert, with a palpable 'sons of Iceland' atmosphere surrounding it, creating an unforgettable experience. 'I saw a white light that was not of this world, all the muscles of my body tensed for a split second, and when they relaxed, an indescribable shiver ran through me. Tears ran down my right cheek, and I squeezed the hand of the person next to me,' said Atli Bollason in his review of the concert in *Morgunblaðið*, which bore the headline 'The best thing God has created'.

Following the success of *Takk...* Sigur Rós concluded a prosperous journey with heartfelt, intimate concerts all around the country in July and August 2006, culminating in a grand concert in Miklatún Park, which lies just east of Reykjavík's downtown area. Admission to these concerts was free, and this, along with various other elements that diverged from typical pop industry norms, solidified the band's status as one of the most significant groups to have ever operated here.

The Icelandic concerts gave rise to the film *Heima* (Home), the band's ode to their native country, released in 2007. Mesmerizing, beautiful, otherworldly, Icelandic . . . yes, but in a fairytale-like manner. Truthful, engaging and inspired, but inevitably fodder for the press seeking to portray Iceland as a Neverland. The film quickly attained a cult-like status and has been the subject of numerous academic explorations.

> Iceland's extraordinary natural beauty is as much a star of the movie as Sigur Rós's magisterial music and the all-local crew could hardly have done a more impressive promotional job had 'Heima' been commissioned by the Icelandic Tourist Board itself . . . as rock movies go, this provides an atypically intense – and enormously pleasurable – experience.[5]

Sigur Rós had now become established superstars, at least within the realm of alternative music. Demigods, even (music tourists, tattooed with the band's logos and symbols, go for a pilgrimage of sorts to Iceland, hoping to meet their idols). In 2008 Sigur Rós released their fifth album, *Með suð í eyrum við spilum endalaust* (With a Buzz in Our Ears We Play Endlessly), which was quite a poppy affair, deliberately toning down the seriousness, more so than on *Takk...* The last song, 'All Alright', was the first in which they sang in English (the rest of the album's lyrics were in Icelandic). The album was produced in an almost garage-like style, and no other Sigur Rós album had been completed in such a short time – just two months, all in all.[6]

This approach to working also extended to the album's cover, which featured a photograph by Ryan McGinley, a promising young photographer from New York. The cover intentionally diverged from the band's previous designs, highlighting simplicity and a sort of vibe of disposability. The CD case was a basic paper one, further emphasizing the throwaway concept. Bassist Georg Holm explained that as people increasingly store music on computers, the physical disc itself becomes a relic that may even be lost.[7] We could say that Sigur Rós foresaw the disappearance of physical music objects years before it became a widespread reality. The decade closed with a sort of hiatus and Jónsi released a solo album in 2010 (*Go*). We will catch up with the band again in the 2020s chapter, taking stock of their activities in the 2010s and '20s.

The other 'breaking news' in the home-grown avant-garde music that found a somewhat unexpected audience abroad was the indietronica collective múm. Formed in 1997 at the Menntaskólinn við Hamrahlíð, the group comprised Gunnar Örn Tynes, Örvar Þóreyjarson Smárason, and twin sisters Gyða Valtýsdóttir and Kristín Anna Valtýsdóttir (only sixteen years old at the time). They were all multi-instrumentalists and the music portrayed on the first three albums (*Yesterday Was Dramatic – Today Is OK* (1999), *Finally We Are No One* (2002) and *Summer Make Good* (2004)) was a wonder to behold.

Imbued with a sense of whimsy and nostalgia, múm evokes an innocent, imagined past. The music is reminiscent of twee heroes like The Pastels and Belle and Sebastian while incorporating the glitchy electronic soundscapes of the Warp label. Their sonic tapestry is quite unique, featuring ethereal vocals, electronic textures and a diverse array of traditional and experimental instruments that float in and out of earshot.

Photogenic indietronica act múm at the Galtarviti lighthouse in 2002, where their third album, *Summer Make Good* (2004), was partially recorded.

Seeing them on stage in Iceland in 2004 was like entering a dream world; quiet and reserved musicians on the stage walking freely between instruments, conjuring up a magical world:

> I felt as if I were in a scene from *Mary Poppins* when I glanced up at the stage in the small but ever so cozy Bæjarbíó . . . There was a Victorian allure about it. Trunks, old gramophones, and abandoned lamps adorned it, shimmering shadows on velvet curtains, darting between the array of instruments; violins, trumpets, organs, drums, and bells. Just like the aforementioned movie, the evening was about to be enchanted by magic.[8]

múm's reputation grew through record releases on respected labels such as Fat Cat (which also released music by Sigur Rós) and the Berlin-based Morr Music. Tours in Europe in the first half of the decade cemented their status. The band's association with these influential labels and their successful tours helped them reach a wider audience and solidify their position in the international alternative music scene.

It is evident that this decade began with numerous bands and musicians following the path initially paved by Björk, then propelled by GusGus and finally expanded even further by Sigur Rós. The doors were now wide open, attracting the attention of foreign managers, the press and record labels, all eager and enthusiastic about the 'new sounds' from Iceland. The Icelandic popular music phenomenon was a fact. Leaves was one of the bands that emerged during this time, a band that could be seen as a post-Radiohead group, releasing an album titled *Breathe* in the UK in 2002. Arnar Guðjónsson, a veteran of the Icelandic 1990s death metal scene, was now 24, the age when pop musicians create their masterpieces. He and his friend Hallur Már were renting an apartment in downtown Reykjavík and began crafting songs together. The band's beginnings were very 'bedsit', with the subdued vocals on their initial release, the song 'Breathe', stemming from Arnar recording quietly in his parents' house to avoid disturbing them.[9]

Leaves then made inroads into the UK music scene, sharing stages with bands like The Coral and Doves, receiving rave reviews. DreamWorks in the USA subsequently released their album there in 2003. Leaves had the music and their next album, *The Angela Test* (2005), was even better than their impressive debut. However, global fame sadly eluded the band, a fate shared by so many who engage in the major label lottery. The band continued at a semi-regular level, releasing albums in their home country. Arnar is now one of the most sought-after record producers in Iceland but he continues to create music as well, both solo and with bands, including work for television and film.

One artist who made a notable impact internationally this decade was Emilíana Torrini. Her debut album, *Love in the Time of Science* (1999), managed to establish her as an international star, a position she has maintained to this day. While releases may be sporadic, her status remains unscathed. She first caught the public eye in 1994 when she won a school talent competition with Gloria Gaynor's 'I Will Survive'. Subsequently, Emilíana collaborated with Jón Ólafsson of Nýdönsk on two albums primarily consisting of cover songs.[10] *Crouçie d'où là* (1995) and *Merman* (1996) established Emilíana as an important figure in the Icelandic music scene, selling a combined total of 18,000 copies. During this period, Emilíana also demonstrated a more exploratory side, collaborating with the indie rock band Slowblow and participating in the making of the first album by the GusGus collective. In 1998 Emilíana relocated abroad, first to London and then to Brighton. Around this time she began laying the groundwork for a solo album, aimed at the international market. The album was tailored to an audience unfamiliar with Emilíana's work back home, where she was primarily seen as a pop star. The record featured an epic, dramatic pop sound, relatively slow-paced and devoid of obvious hits. To emphasize this, the first single, 'Dead Things', had an appropriately brown-toned cover. The album was a collaborative effort, with notable contributions from various artists, including Roland Orzabal from British pop duo Tears for Fears who served as the main producer and contributed to the songwriting. Additionally, Eg White played an important role, alongside Icelanders Sigtryggur Baldursson and Jóhann Jóhannsson. In 2000 efforts were made to market the singer in Europe and the USA, with a focus on long-term success by taking a slow and steady approach. In April that year, Emilíana opened for Sting and performed at concerts across Europe and the USA.[11]

Emilíana then engaged in various high-profile activities. She contributed a track to a Paul Oakenfold album and sang 'Gollum's Song', the title track of the second instalment of Peter Jackson's *Lord of the Rings* trilogy. In 2003 Emilíana and her collaborator, Dan Carey, co-wrote a song for Kylie Minogue titled 'Slow'. The song became the lead single from Minogue's 2003 album, *Body Language*, and achieved widespread global success. For their work, Emilíana and

Emilíana Torrini enjoys an international career that was ignited in the 2000s.

Carey received a Grammy Award nomination. By this point, Emilíana had switched record labels, parting ways with One Little Independent and Virgin, and signed with the renowned Rough Trade.

When *Fisherman's Woman* was released in 2005, it received almost unanimous praise from critics, and that year Emilíana continued to rise in international popularity. Instead of the grand, epic pop songs, Emilíana had shifted to a low-key, intimate album with a folk-like quality, haunting in its nature, flowing along like one long lullaby. In 2008 Emilíana released another album, *Me And Armini*, yet again with Carey on the consoles. The album threads the needle between accessible pop, carried by Emilíana's voice, and somewhat darker, more artistic musings. The third single, the infectious 'Jungle Drum', quickly became very popular and reigned at the top of the German charts for a whopping eight weeks. It can be asserted that no other Icelandic musician has achieved such success.

Even if Emilíana and Leaves didn't particularly emphasize their Icelandic roots, their qualities were associated with Sigur Rós and múm by the foreign press and subsequently simplified and exaggerated. The concept of the 'Icelandic' musician – a lava-field-trotting, wool-sweater-wearing creature – began to emerge and firmly establish itself in the foreign press during this decade. The foundation had been laid in the 1990s, and now it was solidified and hardened.

Strong scenes swept through the Icelandic popular music culture like blizzards at the beginning of the 2000s. In 1999 a band called Mínus won Músíktilraunir. Their music was merciless metalcore, which followed hardcore developments in the USA (Earth Crisis, Converge, the Victory Records label). With shaved heads, basketball tees, caps, skater shoes and loose-fit Dickies trousers, Mínus took the competition by storm (led by Krummi Björgvinsson, the son of pop star Björgvin Halldórsson). An Icelandic metal/hardcore scene was born, a scene that lasted until circa 2002. Mínus spearheaded it with a series of ever-evolving and increasingly impressive albums. Their debut, *Hey Johnny!* (1999), contains brutal metalcore; hard, fast and relentlessly crunching songs. Not resting on their laurels, two years later saw the onslaught of *Jesus Christ Bobby*, a mind-bendingly experimental metalcore album produced by noisenik producer Curver. In 2003 their masterpiece *Halldór Laxness* was released, named cheekily after Iceland's best-known author, clearly showing the self-esteem that the band had at the time. The music drew inspiration from classic hard rock, Motörhead and Guns N' Roses, while blending in elements of metalcore and psychedelic rock. Mind-blowing stuff. The band ventured abroad, touring Europe and seeing the album released by Sony and its subsidiaries on the continent.

The scene that drove Mínus to success had its roots established slightly before their triumph in Músíktilraunir. In the years circa 1997 and 1998, legendary bands like Bisund and Spitsign were in action, the latter hinting in places at the fury of nu-metallers like Korn. Interestingly, a nu-metal scene never took hold in Iceland. A number of bands flooded the scene in the wake of Mínus's rise and a strong community evolved, having a home base of sorts on an Internet

Hardcore kings Mínus in 1998, the year the band was formed.

discussion board hosted by the website Dordingull and simply called Taflan (the Board). There within, friendships were forged and the scene kept alive. Bands like Elexír, Snafu, Vígspá, Andlát and the mighty Klink did the 'heavy' lifting scene-wise while I Adapt played melodic, call-to-arms hardcore in the vein of Minor Threat.[12]

In some ways, the scene had little commonality with earlier extreme rock scenes like punk or death metal. All those scenes, more or less, were responding to new and exciting music from abroad and, as detailed in the 1980s chapter, a response to punk music was delayed, while the death metal scene ran almost in parallel with other scenes of that type. This home-brewed hardcore/metal scene recalled the death metal scene in terms of being in line with foreign developments, if just a little delayed. But what distanced it from those two scenes were certain social factors: Taflan along with culinary and environmental politics, derived from the straight edge philosophy, for instance.[13] Feminist views that were found in very small doses – albeit powerful ones – in the punk scene, but had completely bypassed the death metal scene, made an entrance in this one, mostly audience-wise. The bands were all male-led, with only one or two exceptions. There were also significant outliers, bands that were like islands, with no scene to adhere to *sans* the general rock atmosphere that the hardcore bands undeniably brought with them. Desert/stoner rockers Brain Police have royalty status today, selling out every show when they tune up for their regular comebacks. Kimono, an Icelandic-Canadian math rock band, and Graveslime, a sludge-rock band in the mould of Melvins, also made their mark.

Another scene made a huge impact around the same time. Hip-hop arrived late to Iceland, very late in fact, compared to the beat group scene of the 1960s, the punk scene of the 1980s (and that arrived quite late, as has been detailed) or the death metal scene. Throughout the 1980s, rap had been developing abroad, but no one in Iceland was paying much attention, making their own beats or practising their flow. It wasn't until well into the 1990s that Icelanders began to embrace it and the first groups to do so were quite different from one another (touched upon in the 1990s chapter). In 1996 the band Quarashi released the 'Switchstance' EP, which featured powerful rap-rock, and a year later the multicultural posse Subterranean released the album *Central Magnetizm*. It drew heavily from American hip-hop but what it lacked in originality was made up for with youthful passion. These two bands were mostly isolated entities and stood apart from the full-blown hip-hop scene that flourished a few years later.

In 2000 the rap group 110 Rottweilerhundar (110 Rottweiler Dogs) won the Músíktilraunir competition. The number 110 referred to the postal code of the neighbourhood that spawned the group

(Árbæjarhverfi) but later they changed 110 to XXX. The neighbourhood, incidentally where this author grew up, is located on the far east side of Reykjavík. It is a small, leafy and calm suburb. South of Árbær lies Breiðholt, Reykjavík's largest suburb. To the north is Grafarvogur, another large suburb. All these neighbourhoods began to develop in the 1970s and '80s, when Reykjavík was rapidly expanding in population. The group's victory, and their debut album released the following year, caused nothing less than a revolution in Icelandic hip-hop and the resulting movement is referred to as its first wave. The most important thing about the arrival of Rottweilerhundar is that they rapped in Icelandic, something that had not been done properly before. On the contrary, many believed that it was impossible to rap in Icelandic, that it would be ridiculous and would not work rhythmically or musically. This attitude changed overnight with the posse's win.

XXX Rottweilerhundar were provocative and powerful, young Icelanders who expressed what was on their minds in Icelandic – everyday troubles and challenges, like the sociorealism of Spilverk þjóðanna or the rebellious lyrics of the punk rock groups; straight from the ghetto in a way, rhymes about crime, sex and forbidden things, partly detailing the realities of the Reykjavík suburban youth, partly aping a gangsta style from the USA. There was an explosion of activity among Icelandic rappers in the aftermath and the first wave lasted until around 2003. Quarashi achieved great success abroad when their 2002 album *Jinx*, released internationally by Columbia, went on to sell 500,000 copies worldwide. From 2003 onwards, the first wave began to evaporate quite quickly. The second wave then began in 2015 with Gísli Pálmi's debut album.[14] More about that in the 2010s chapter.

One notable scene that emerged during this decade, the third one deserving special mention, is what we could term 'all-Icelandic pop'. This genre had minimal ties, or none whatsoever, to passing trends and fashions in foreign countries; it was a distinctly home-grown phenomenon but built on former, similar scenes (detailed in the 1990s chapter). Its primary aim was to create radio-friendly music, suitable for social gatherings (the country dances) and to break into the mainstream pop scene where fame and fortune beckoned. At first, the scene was strictly rural. The forerunners were a band established in the Western region, in a small town called Stykkishólmur. Vinir vors og blóma (Friends of Spring and Flowers) ran from 1993 to 1996, playing said dances and releasing poppy albums in the summertime (always in the summertime). This mantle was then carried on and advanced by a band hailing from Selfoss, the capital of South Iceland. Skítamórall (Shitty Attitude) played cheerful, catchy pop that quickly found an audience, releasing their debut album in 1996.[15] The band were driven, with a Beatles-esque, gang-like presence, like all the charming, breakthrough bands of yore. Style was not lost on them either, a 1990s anime-inspired boy band look, squarely and meticulously over the top. All of this worked neatly in their favour.

Rap-rock outfit Quarashi found fame abroad in the 2000s, especially in the USA.

Skítamórall pioneered this all-out pop rebirth, deeply influenced by earlier kings like Sálin hans Jóns míns. The bands that became most prominent around the turn of the century were effectively filling the void left by the late 1980s/early 1990s pop bands. Skítamórall and Land og synir (Land and Sons) vied for the spotlight along with Á móti sól (Against the Sun), all from the south. The scene reached its peak in 2000, with Írafár (Flurry) and Í svörtum fötum (In Black Clothes) quickly joining the ranks along with Buttercup and Sóldögg (Sundew). The 'second-wave' bands in this millenium pop onslaught had stronger connections to the capital, with some originating solely from the city, highlighting the scene's outreach.[16] While it's uncommon for Reykjavík bands to draw inspiration from rural areas, it does happen (a similar situation arose in the 1960s of course, when Hljómar led the beat boom).

Interestingly, when it came to album-making the bands stroked their chins rather than shaking their legs and as the scene wound on, we saw quite ambitious album-making, laced with experiments and attempts at creating worthwhile album tunes (not dissimilar to the bands of the 1980s and '90s). A hit was appreciated, but a respectable track record as serious musicians was as well. Írafár dominated the scene as it started to wind down (the singer, Birgitta, even had a children's doll styled after her) and around 2004 the scene dissolved.

This brings us to Einar Bárðarson, known as 'Iceland's Svengali', who managed to reach for the stars – sometimes literally – during this decade. This author documented his adventures in his very first book, *Umboðsmaður Íslands: Öll trixin í bókinni* (Iceland's Svengali: All the Tricks in the Book), in 2007.[17] Einar came from the south, like the pop-scene instigators detailed above, and had strong ties to that scene. For instance, he wrote Skítamórall's very first hit – his brother was and still is a guitarist in the band. A natural wheeler and dealer, his management tactics took off when he drew inspiration from the boy and girl group scene of the late 1990s and early 2000s, leading

Skítamórall led the charge in the renewal of all-Icelandic pop music in the 2000s.

to the creation of the girl band Nylon. That ball started rolling after Einar's song 'Angel', performed by the duo Two Tricky, won the preliminary round of the Eurovision Song Contest in Iceland in 2001, allowing it to compete in the main event in Copenhagen later that year. Einar was now slowly but surely amassing both experience and contacts related to all things pop marketing. In early 2004 he began laying the groundwork for Nylon. This venture took him to London, where he settled, opened an office and established a record label

Á móti sól, one of the high-flying pop bands of the 2000s.

and agency, Believer Music. In 2005 Einar started to work with tenor Garðar Thor Cortes and launched his career both at home and abroad (his album, *Cortes*, became the best-selling classical album in the UK for a period).[18] In 2007 Einar inaugurated yet another project, the singing group Luxor (in the style of Il Divo), which was short-lived. He was involved in many projects after that, music-related and not, but has now returned 'home' and is the chairman of the board at the new and expanded Iceland Music (Tónlistarmiðstöð in Icelandic, literally 'music centre'), established in 2023 and serving as an umbrella organization where 'the entirety of music in Iceland has found a permanent home where education, support and information are available in one place.'[19]

One of the most beloved bands in the local scene during this decade was Hjálmar, a reggae group hailing from Keflavík. Hjálmar, meaning 'helmets' in Icelandic (also a masculine given name), released two albums in 2004 and 2005, performed numerous concerts and gained widespread popularity in a short period of time. Their songs became fixtures on daytime radio, drawing admiration both from hipsters and the general public. With first-class musicianship, where the band played as one man on stage, and with some uniquely Icelandic, indescribable touches on the reggae form, the band managed to captivate everyone.

The origins of Hjálmar can be traced back to two musicians, Sigurður Halldór Guðmundsson and Guðm. Kristinn Jónsson, known as Siggi and Kiddi Hjálmur. After collaborating on various projects, Hjálmar's debut album was recorded in just a week, featuring radio-friendly tunes, some odd pieces and some cover songs. The album fell on fertile ground, owing not only to the band's irresistible magic but to the exceptional quality of the music itself, characterized by a rich, well-crafted sound. A year later, an eponymous album followed suit, now with a lineup consisting of three Icelanders and three Swedes. This sophomore album was even better than its predecessor, showcasing what the band members themselves dubbed as 'wool sweater reggae', a style accentuated both by the album's cover and the musical texture – a blend of Icelandic and Swedish influences infused into a reggae template. This theme was further reinforced by the album's marvellous opening track, a reggae rendition of an old Swedish folk song. During this time, the band performed with a synergy they had never experienced before and the unity and intimacy among the members started to manifest in a way that was separate from their music.[20] Consequently, the members began to mirror each other in appearance, all donning hippy beards, wool sweaters and moccasins, leading one to envision them unwinding together in a nearby commune – a scenario not far from reality.[21] The band called it quits in August 2006, simply exhausted. They regrouped in 2007 and have been operating on and off to this day.

Hjálmar's career laid the foundation for a group of musicians involved in diverse projects that were mostly carried out between 2005 and 2015. This collective, known as Memfismafían (the Memphis Mafia), derived its name from the renowned Hljóðriti studios mentioned in Chapter Three.[22] The mafia worked on children's records, crooner albums (featuring Siggi), Christmas albums and more, all of which gained immense popularity. Their production process had a Motown-like feel, with products released in quick succession and always of the highest quality. This approach was also reminiscent of how Rúnar Júlíusson and Spilverkið/Stuðmenn/Þursar did their thing in the 1970s, and Kiddi and Siggi hail from the same town as Rúnar (with him serving as a mentor to both).

Many of these musicians were also members of the Baggalútur band. The Baggalútur project started as a group of college friends sharing jokes on an Internet platform in the mid-1990s. As the web page gained popularity, it led to the release of a full album in 2005, produced by Kiddi. Subsequent albums featured humorous, homely and distinctly Icelandic content that found audiences easily. Today, Baggalútur's Christmas concerts are among the most popular in Iceland, with sold-out shows and support from various members of Hjálmar and Memfismafían. The Midas touch of these two friends from Keflavík has shaped mainstream Icelandic music considerably over the past two decades. Additionally, I must mention Senuþjófarnir (The Scene Stealers), a band from the same circle that collaborated with and supported Megas in recording albums and touring.[23]

We will keep our ears firmly to the Icelandic ground for a while. Two artists, Mugison (Örn Elías Guðmundsson) and Jónas Sig (Jónas Sigurðsson), embody a deeply etched Icelandic identity that gets a thumbs-up from your grandmother but is simultaneously approved by the chin-stroking crowd. They became highly popular within

Iceland, and similar to Hjálmar's situation, achieving worldwide fame was neither a starting point nor a goal in itself.

Mugison emerged out of thin air. A CD demo/promo in a hand-scribbled cardboard sleeve stood on my desk at *Morgunblaðið* for many months before I bothered to check it out. The album was *Lonely Mountain*, Mugison's first album proper, released in 2002. The album garnered much attention among music enthusiasts, containing a uniquely enchanting blend of melodic pop and electronic buzz. It originated when Mugison lived in London and was released through Matthew Herbert's Accidental label. To Mugison's despair, Herbert also loved the packaging of the demo he was handed – a handmade paper case stitched together with a needle and thread. So, Mugison spent the following year stitching 13,000 copies of *Lonely Mountain* together. Mugison then moved to the Westfjords and started work on *Mugimama Is this Monkey Music?* (2004), an album that shot him into the Icelandic stratosphere. 'A talented musician, yes, but it was not least his personality that seemed to touch the Icelandic nation at its core, embracing his refreshing eccentricity and unpretentiousness. The interviews were characterized by effortless charm.'[24] Here was an artist who was well connected in hip music circles abroad yet exuded a diligent, down-to-earth vibe at the same time. Embodying a rural Icelander engaged in musical self-sufficiency, performing at a trendy club in London on a Monday and then at a countryside church in the Westfjords the following day.

Mugimama was mostly recorded in a church in Súðavík, a municipality of around 250 people, where Mugison had moved to live with his girlfriend (she being the 'Mugimama' in question). Various houses in Ísafjörður, the Westfjord capital, were utilized for recordings but the set-up was minimal and the album was almost entirely recorded through a single microphone. Mugison and his friend Pétur Ben would meet at his home, have coffee and churn out songs, as Mugison would put it.[25] A specific rule was set for the album's production, allowing only friends and family members to participate, no hired

Mugison, Örn Elías Guðmundsson, a charismatic troubadour for modern times, loved by grandmothers and hipsters alike.

professionals. Mugison has described the album as somewhat of a family record, with his wife Rúna and his grandfather playing a role, among others.[26]

The outcome was a masterfully peculiar record. The lo-fi aesthetics adorned both the cover and the music, which was characterized by skewed blues songs, beautiful ballads and completely 'out-there' tracks (think Will Oldham, Badly Drawn Boy and Beck). Upon its release, the album received incredible acclaim, praised by all who listened to it. Mugison had now become a household name, world-famous in Iceland as it's called. His next album, *Mugiboogie* (2007), was recorded with a band, Mugison transitioning from a computer troubadour of sorts to a fleshed-out rocker. The album is fat and sweaty – still infused with the Mugi-magic – sounding like The Allman Brothers stranded in a Westfjord tundra.[27]

In 2011 Mugison released his most beloved album, *Haglél* (Hailstorm). This was a simple, delicately crafted song-based album that echoed, at times, the classic 1970s Icelandic pop style of Mannakorn and Spilverkið. 'I wanted to make a bad Mannakorn album,' Mugison quipped, showcasing his typically wry, self-deprecating humour. The album was released in the autumn and achieved sales exceeding 30,000 units. All the songs were in Icelandic, recorded with friends in different homes and makeshift studios. As a token of appreciation to those who purchased the album he organized three complimentary concerts in December 2011, which took place in the recently opened Harpa concert hall in Reykjavík (more on Harpa in the next chapter). As usual, the cover was handmade, making the production of 30,000 copies a full-time endeavour for his friends and family. One of my last assignments at *Morgunblaðið*, when I was still a staffer, was to write a review of that album:

> Another song from the album, 'Stingum af', is perhaps the best example of its spirit. Over the catchy melody, Mugison sings about all those little things that make life worth living, things

> we can all relate to. This is where the strength of the album lies; by baring himself to the core, Mugison manages to touch us like never before.[28]

And touch people this particular song did, becoming quite the anthem in the following months and still a 'lighters in the air' moment at his concerts.[29]

Jónas Sig (Jónas Sigurðsson) has had quite an interesting career. Originally from the south and a drummer at the time, he went to college in the east, where he performed with garage bands but played paid gigs at the country dances as well. In 1995 a joke duet, Sólstrandargæjarnir (The Beach Guys), engineered by Einar Bárðarson at the very start, became an overnight sensation, and they ran with it for the next year. Disorientated, Jónas abruptly quit music in 1996 and deliberately kept out of the public eye, doing dead-end jobs for a few years. He then learnt computer programming, which landed him a job with Microsoft in Denmark and greener pastures suddenly beckoned in the USA. Unable to shrug off his musical need, he released a solo album for the Icelandic market in 2006, while still living in Denmark. The album was met with much critical acclaim, effectively jump-starting his music career for a second time. And just like in Mugison's case, the album struck a fine balance between appealing pop and more eccentric ventures. Now wiser and more content, Jónas has since built a respectable music career in his home country, enjoying quite some success, and has been able to build a bridge between an indie audience and the mainstream crowd.[30] He and Mugison even formed a band with guitar virtuoso Ómar Guðjónsson in 2013. Called Drangar, they travelled around the country that same year.

There's a folky undercurrent in Drangar's music as well as in Mugison's. In this decade, a few artists with that strand of music-making as their baseline emerged. It's a bit difficult to detect it; folk music, whether from the USA, the UK or the Scandinavian regions, has long been an integral aspect of Icelandic music-making, as detailed in the preceding chapters. However, Icelandic folk music has been regarded by Icelandic popular musicians as a museum artefact mostly, rather than a fundamental part of their musical identity. Remarkably, modern, domestic folk musicians who have made any impact mostly use either American (country blues, Appalachian folk) or English folk as their inspiration.[31]

In 2006 an album was released that introduced us to a folk supernova. *Please Don't Hate Me* by Lay Low (Lovísa Elísabet Sigrúnardóttir) was one of the earliest local examples of the MySpace phenomenon, as she had been uploading her songs to that site for a while. A new label, COD music (which was under the wings of Sena, the major label), immediately signed her up. The album gained traction in sales and a chord was struck that appealed to both seasoned music aficionados and casual listeners (like so many of the artists that 'make it' in Iceland; KK, Mugison and others). The music is an eclectic blend of blues, country and folk, sung with a unique vocal style reminiscent of American blues singers from the 1960s and '70s, exuding a low-key charm. This success started a career and the next album, the countrified *Farewell Good Night's Sleep* (2008), was aimed at foreign markets, where Lay Low performed at Glastonbury Festival and toured with Emilíana Torrini. In 2012 she supported Of Monsters and Men on their USA tour (more about them in the next chapter) and although her last album was released in 2015, she remains a household name in Iceland and performs regularly.

At the end of the decade, Snorri Helgason stepped forward with the solo album *I'm Gonna Put My Name on Your Door*. Snorri had made a name for himself as one of the members of Sprengjuhöllin (The Bomb Palace), but folk music ran in his bloodline as well, as he was the son of one of the Ríó tríó members (Helgi Pétursson, Helgi P.). The album has a Dylanesque vibe to it, especially in the cover design, which recalled American singer-songwriter heroes from the late 1960s and early 1970s. The music is a blend of folk, rock and soul with song titles like 'Carol' and 'Queen Street', and Snorri's deep love for that era is obvious. His later albums were both folky and not so folky but his fifth album, *Margt býr í þokunni* (What Lurks in the Fog), was a pure embrace of Icelandic folk music heritage.

Another central figure, folk-wise, is Svavar Knútur, who embarked on a singer-songwriter career at the end of the last decade with the album *Kvöldvaka* (Songs by the Fire, 2009). Leading up to that, he had played in a variety of groups. His style is heartfelt and sincere, yet never devoid of humorous observations, and you can detect Nick Drake and Will Oldham as influences. His sophomore album, *Amma* (Songs for My Grandmother), was recorded in his best friend's living room in front of a group of family and close friends. In recent years, Svavar Knútur has toured Australia, the USA, Canada, Great Britain and Europe extensively, successfully establishing himself in the international market as well as on his home turf. The same can be said of Árstíðir (Seasons), a band who began their journey around the same time. Characterized by the harmony singing of its three members, the band managed to establish themselves on foreign soil, attracting audiences with their blend of folk-like elements and contemporary nuances. In a similar fashion to the Faroe Islands' Eivör, an alluring, Nordic folk-like aura is packaged effectively and Árstíðir has a strong international fan base that has crowdfunded half of the band's eight-album discography.[32]

The singer-songwriter genre in Iceland is a sizeable one, always active, but barely noticeable in a way when we focus on the broader strokes in Icelandic popular music history. Bubbi is the king but, of course, there's a steady stream throughout the year of individuals with a guitar, both forgettable and unforgettable, releasing their music as albums or not at all. I could mention Bergþóra Árnadóttir, who made a notable impact in the 1970s with her protest-laden songs. I can reel off names like Siggi Björns, Halli Reynis, Teitur and Bjarni Tryggva, all of them worthy of a mention, or the great Orri Harðarson who released magnificent albums in the 1990s. Or Songbird, Nanna

Bryndís of Of Monsters and Men's troubadour moniker. But this is not a phone book.

In the mid-2000s a curious development took place. Shedding light on this is best achieved by describing a popular band, Retro Stefson. The band comprised six members at the beginning, all born around 1990, including the brothers Unnsteinn Manuel Stefánsson (lead vocal, guitar and the de facto leader of the group) and Logi Pedro Stefánsson (bass). The brothers spent the first few years of their lives in Portugal, living with their Icelandic father and Angolan mother. The band quickly earned a reputation as a prodigious live act, playing joyous indie rock with a stage presence to match. In the summer of 2008, the band recorded its first album, *Montaña*, containing a colourful music platter laid with indie pop/rock and then heaped with bossa nova, disco, jazz and whatever else a creative teenager, who still doesn't know or recognize the aesthetic rules of pop music-making, sees fit to play around with. Additionally, Retro Stefson's music tapped into a certain reactionary evolution in Icelandic indie rock that began around 2005. In a way it was derived from important Icelandic indie/underground/avant-garde bands like Sigur Rós, múm and Slowblow, a magnificent band that was built on the remnants of Rosebud. While certain attitudes from these bands were inherited, the texture of the music that Retro Stefson began producing was quite different. Notably absent, for example, was the often studied seriousness and reserved demeanour of said bands. While those artists were introverted, Retro Stefson and the other artists who they often travelled and shared stages with (for example FM Belfast, Sprengjuhöllin and Jeff Who?) were extroverted. Sigur Rós had considerable qualms, especially at the beginning, with the commercialism surrounding the making of modern pop and rock music, but this aspect was of no concern to Retro's generation. The order of the day was campy fun and lively tunes, grounded in the indie rocker's outlook, and if fame came knocking at the door, it was welcomed with hearty greetings.

Sprengjuhöllin played radio-friendly pop with clever, literate lyrics. They were campy and humorous in interviews, sometimes coming across as prickly loudmouths, but undeniably charming at the same time. Stuðmenn vibes. FM Belfast opted for electro-pop and became known for their legendary, party-filled concerts. They were the band you would want to hire to close the Airwaves festival, or any festival for that matter.[33] Jeff Who? played happy-go-lucky pop/rock, with their frontman exuding easy-going charisma to the maximum. In hindsight, all of this seems a natural reaction to a certain 'seriousness fatigue'. Another band galloping the music scene with a knowing wink was Trabant, which comprised luminaries from the 1990s alt-rock and death metal scenes. Their 2006 album

Retro Stefson were one of the pioneers of an exuberant, joyous scene in the mid-2000s, partly in response to the seriousness of Sigur Rós and their fellow travellers.

Emotional made an impact at the time and the singer was one Ragnar Kjartansson, the internationally renowned artist.

Hjaltalín were a world of their own – more serious than the aforementioned bands but far from the avant-garde rule book at the same time, at least in the beginning. Soon enough, a boundless ambition was apparent in this unique band who started their flight in 2007 with the chamber-pop of debut album *Sleepdrunk Seasons*. The album received high praise from critics who could hardly contain their excitement over the flawless fusion of pop and classical elements found within. The band was established at Menntaskólinn við Hamrahlíð in the autumn of 2004 in connection with a songwriting competition organized by the school's student association. The momentum for the band then built up steadily until the release of their sophomore album, *Terminal* (2009). Even more ambitious than the debut, all shackles were now broken and the band roamed freely with their breathtaking interpretation of popular music and its possibilities. Yes, that album is a true masterpiece, containing epic chamber pop, reminiscent of Scott Walker at the height of his power. While *Sleepdrunk Seasons* was linear in its flow, *Terminal* jumps up and down. It's big, dramatic, relentless. As this author wrote at the time: 'An incredibly mature and passionate work . . . This versatile band has delivered a true masterpiece, a work that continues to grow and stir my head. A true tour de force when all is said and done, simply put, a magnificent creation.'[34] The next album, *Enter 4*, was released in 2012, a dark and deep affair where the avant-garde-ism was turned up to the max. The members have almost all pursued solo careers, as singers, producers and composers. The band's legacy also lies in the skill of allowing their music education (all of them had degrees under their belts) to serve creativity. There was never any unnecessary nonsense or pretence, gimmicks or gamesmanship. The music itself directed.

Benni Hemm Hemm (Benedikt Hermann Hermannsson) was another important musician who, just like Hjaltalín, skilfully utilized his music education. He has released attractive, accessible music but also boundary-pushing experiments. After stints with various bands, he released a six-track solo record in 2003 (*Summerplate*, a 3-inch CD of which only thirty copies were produced), and the band Benni Hemm Hemm first performed the following year. The music then often resembled chamber pop, but with Benedikt's unique twist. Benni's career is ongoing and albums are released at regular intervals, with all kinds of approaches. In the mid-2000s there were also rock groups such as Mammút (Mammoth), who emerged victorious at Músíktilraunir in 2004. Their album releases progressively improved in quality and the band eventually ventured into the export market. Morðingjarnir (The Murderers) presented a melodic power-trio punk rock sound, characterized by an impressive blend of sharp lyricism and socio-realistic reflections, the band sharing a bed with Pixies, S.H. Draumur and Hüsker Dü. The brilliantly named Reykjavík! and the maniacal live favourites Sudden Weather Change were also fine contributors to the sweaty side of things this decade. Agent Fresco won Músíktilraunir in 2008, bringing in polyrhythmic progressive rock where brutal sections were broken up by angelic runs from mesmerizing singer Arnór. The band reflected international fashions in heavy music and managed to brush the mainstream, releasing fine albums in 2010 and 2015 while maintaining a reputation as one of Iceland's foremost live draws.

Lastly, even if just to emphasize the versatility on hand, we must mention Jakobínarína, the winners of the 2005 edition of Músíktilraunir. Playing sprightly indie pop, the members were just fourteen and fifteen years old when the band started. After the win, they were jettisoned to the UK, released a 7-inch single on Rough Trade and signed an album deal with Regal Records, an imprint of Parlophone. Tours and live concerts were set up and the teenagers from Hafnarfjörður soon found themselves in an unruly maelstrom that eventually washed them back up on Icelandic shores, half eaten by the industry machine. This author interviewed the members for

Morgunblaðið in 2008, a few days after a split announcement, lending a sympathetic ear to the trials and tribulations of eighteen-year-old rock retirees.[35] Frontman Gunnar Ragnarsson later formed Grísalappalísa, a more artistic affair that garnered rave reviews, both live and as a recording unit. But the market was squarely domestic this time around.[36]

In this decade, Jóhann Jóhannsson's career took flight, and he would go on to be one of Iceland's best-known and respected musicians on the international stage. As a score composer for theatre and films, and as a solo artist, he spanned a wide spectrum, from mainstream OSTs (original soundracks) to more experimental works. He peaked in the mid-2010s when the celebrated Icelandic film composer scene had become a reality. Beside Jóhann, there was Academy-Award winner Hildur Guðnadóttir, author of the lauded *Chernobyl* OST and the *Joker* OST. She is the first Icelander to receive an Oscar and only the fourth woman film composer to do so in the history of the almost century-old awards. The much-heralded Ólafur Arnalds, a versatile composer who has worked in various fields, wrote the music for the popular British television series *Broadchurch* and received a BAFTA for his efforts in 2014. Additionally, Hilmar Örn Hilmarsson (HÖH, who worked on 'Hrafnagaldur Óðins' with Sigur Rós) must be mentioned, as he laid the groundwork for all of these successes with his beautiful OST for the Icelandic film *Börn náttúrunnar* (Children of Nature, 1991). Later, he wrote the music for the Icelandic film *Englar alheimsins* (Angels of the Universe), which resulted in a collaboration with Sigur Rós and international renown (the score for Jane Campion's film *In the Cut* (2003) for instance). HÖH originally emerged from the punk scene, working closely with Þeyr, Bad Taste members and UK acts like Current 93 in the 1980s and '90s. Atli Örvarsson has also been industrious; after playing with Sálin hans Jóns míns, he moved to the USA and worked in Hollywood on television and film scores, collaborating with Hans Zimmer among others. In 2016 he moved back to Iceland and set up a studio

Composer Hildur Guðnadóttir is the first Icelander to win an Academy Award, receiving the Oscar for Best Original Score for her work on the film *Joker* (dir. Todd Phillips, 2019).

and a label in his hometown of Akureyri, bringing in projects through his amassed connections from abroad, trying to establish the town as an international destination for film score recording.[37]

It's interesting to note that all of the above have roots in the punk/underground scene of Iceland. Jóhann's credits have been established, Hildur, albeit classically trained, made a name for herself through various indie bands and HÖH's background has been detailed. Ólafur Arnalds had his start in the Icelandic hardcore scene as a drummer. Atli's underground connections are more far-fetched but his first foray into the music scene was through Músíktilraunir, where he and his brother won in 1987 with Stuðkompaníið.

Jóhann Jóhannsson's career as a pioneering modern composer needs a little more detail. The *Englabörn* play score (Angel's Children (2002), on the venerable Touch label) put him on the map along with ever more adventurous solo works: *Virðulegu Forsetar* in 2004

(Respectable Presidents), *IBM 1401, A User's Manual* in 2006, *Fordlandia* in 2008. Ambitious live concerts and, eventually, more film work ensued. The first of these was *Prisoners* (dir. Denis Villeneuve, 2013) and then *The Theory of Everything* (dir. James Marsh, 2014). Accolades followed and Jóhann's talents as well as his music's substance and unique style were becoming apparent to foreign reviewers. His reputation was further solidified by the great OSTs for Denis Villeneuve's *Sicario* (2015) and *Arrival* (2016), as well as *Mandy* (dir. Panos Cosmatos, 2018). Jóhann was incredibly diligent and worked on a variety of projects. He was hired to create the score for another film by Villeneuve, the sequel to 1982's *Blade Runner* titled

Jóhann Jóhannsson carved out an impressive career as a film and post-classical composer that was cut short by his untimely passing in 2018.

Blade Runner 2049 (2017) but his work on that was eventually halted, the director proclaiming: 'The movie needed something different, and I needed to go back to something closer to Vangelis.'[38] The film was eventually scored by Hans Zimmer and Benjamin Wallfisch.

Jóhann was a true musical polymath and boldly blurred lines, crafting a sonic universe that was both distinctive and alluring. His deep understanding of both popular and 'serious' music – and the fact that he was a total film music buff – gave him a unique perspective and his groundbreaking film scores are a testament to this, if nothing else. Jóhann died on 9 February 2018, at 48 years of age, and it sent a shock wave of sadness and grief through the Icelandic music scene. Too much, too young, too soon.

I conclude this chapter by examining some industry developments, starting with the influential label Bedroom Community, which was partly born out of Valgeir Sigurðsson's Greenhouse Studios in the Breiðholt suburb of Reykjavík. The label was established in 2006 and is associated with a 'global collective of artists from different musical and cultural backgrounds, working in new classical, alternative, and experimental music'.[39] The label enjoys a strong international reputation, and both the American composer Nico Muhly and the Australian musician Ben Frost launched their international careers through it. The studio has been utilized by artists such as Will Oldham, Brian Eno, Sigur Rós, Björk, The xx, Damon Albarn, Michael Gira and many others. All of this activity has helped to place Iceland on the map as a musical melting pot, with the label's clear vision serving as an important component in the Icelandic music Mecca wheel. The label has thus been an important hub and a gateway for well-appreciated influx from afar, foreign artists who inevitably bring with them new ideas and directions.

And some of them stay for good: artists who choose to make Iceland their home and the basis for their operations. I'll give an example of three artists. Ben Frost moved to Iceland twenty years ago and has coloured the Icelandic music scene with strong, decisive hues. Frost has a rich, diverse background and has composed music for films, television, theatre and dance performances along with production work, for Icelanders as well as foreign artists. He has collaborated with off-centre giants such as Swans, Steve Albini and Tim Hecker, and his music travels widely across the globe. Damon Albarn of Blur fame started to visit Iceland frequently in the mid-1990s and eventually bought a house here and was granted Icelandic citizenship in 2020. Albarn sung Iceland's praises in the media and made the Kaffibarinn bar (the Coffee Bar) an iconic stopover. He and Einar Örn of the Sugarcubes became good friends, collaborating on projects, and Einar's experimental music project Ghostigital (which became a duet with producer Curver) had its very first release on Honest Jon's, a label co-run by Albarn.[40] The last example is John Grant, who first came to visit in autumn 2011 because of the Icelandic Airwaves festival. He fell hard for the country, even describing the run-down Hlemmur bus station as 'exquisitely beautiful' to this author. He settled permanently in 2013 after hiring Biggi Veira from GusGus to produce his album *Pale Green Ghosts* (featuring a cover that shows him sitting in the legendary Reykjavík coffee house, Mokka).[41] He then recruited some Icelanders to his band. As is clear, these impactful visits benefit both the musical settlers and the musical field they step into.

Just beside Hlemmur is the record store Lucky Records, which began in Kolaportið (Coalyard) flea market in 2005. A fully fledged record store, with a fine second-hand collection and new releases, its establishment was a watershed of its kind. Up to that point, second-hand records were mostly found in the corners of dingy antique bookshops, completely unalphabetized. Trips to London and New York for us Icelandic record collectors were thus like stepping through heaven's gate. Today, Reykjavík prides itself on a commendable variety of record stores: in addition to Lucky Records we have Plötubúðin (The Record Store), Alda Music plötubúð, Bad Taste Record Shop, Reykjavík Record Shop, Hljómsýn, Space Odyssey and Geisladiskabúð Valda (Valdi's CD store). And last but not least, we have 12 Tónar, probably Iceland's most famous record store, known for its inviting atmosphere and quirky interiors. Established in 1998, behind the counter you will find indie legend Einar Sonic, a one-time member of the guitar-wielding rock 'n' roll heroes Singapore Sling.

In the next chapter, we will see how industry advances in the 2010s started to run smoothly, giving way to easier export work and better and stronger connections to foreign markets. This accessibility at least made it possible to work more effectively on foreign ground, for example not having to move away from Iceland if world fame beckoned and for that matter being able to run all operations from Reykjavík, or whatever city or town you might be located in. The domestic market continued to thrive, with more possibilities arising from technological changes (Bandcamp, Spotify and others) and music releases becoming more frequent, along with more collaborations between genres, fortified by the general proximity of Icelandic music life.

7

The 2010s: An Ever-Growing Interest

'No, they are on the Billboard 200, not some indie chart!' a co-worker at *Morgunblaðið* told me in the office's corridors as I was making my way back to my desk after lunch. He was referencing Of Monsters and Men and the release of their debut album, *My Head Is An Animal*, in the USA. 'And they're number six!' I was gutted. Glad, but gutted because I had missed the scoop. I simply had not envisioned that the band that had won Músíktilraunir in 2010 had gotten that far. I had heard a 'little talk' about Billboard but had pushed it away as being a placing in one of the sub-charts.

I was in trouble. I had to have something in the paper. I started to make some calls. I tried to contact the band directly but now it was impossible. It was like they had entered a giant music industry black hole overnight. 'Call this office in Brooklyn,' I was told by someone. Sigh. I rang nephews and mothers with no results. I had to get someone from the band, there was a spread waiting for me in the Sunday edition. I called their Icelandic label manager and a producer they had worked with, to have some quotes ready. My plan B was to have these quotes, a background story, news items and some photos to fill the pages.

But finally, I got one number. A number that belonged to my namesake in the band, drummer Arnar Rósenkranz Hilmarsson. And with roughly three hours to go before the deadline, he picked up. He was aboard a bus, somewhere in the United States, doing a huge tour for the first time in his life, just like the rest of the band. 'You have to pinch yourself,' he said stoically, in between the moments we lost contact as the bus went into a tunnel. The interview was finally in the can but the printing machines had started to roar. I wrote the article speedily and filed my copy circa fifteen minutes before deadline. Phew. We had a worthy piece about this incredible fairy tale that had begun two years earlier when the band won said competition.

In the aftermath of that win, the band played gigs around Iceland and their first record, *My Head Is An Animal*, was released in September 2011 on local label Record Records. 'Arnar and I were both starting school and we were talking about how if something happened, we would just dive right in. Music is our top priority, it is the lifeblood,' Nanna told me just after the release of said debut.[1] In my review for *Morgunblaðið* I wrote:

> The band embraces the new folk wave with influences drawn from bands like Fleet Foxes, Arcade Fire and Bon Iver, to name a few. The songs are joyous and energetic . . . and the musicality is palpable. The music is memorable without being shallow, pleasant to the ear but full of substance. It is no coincidence that it resonates so well on the radio.[2]

A session for KEXP, the influential Seattle radio station, was recorded later in 2011 and a buzz began to spread.[3] The debut album was then released on Republic Records, a subsidiary of Universal Music, on 12 April 2012, resulting in the aforementioned placement in the Billboard 200 top ten. To date, the album has sold over 2 million copies in the USA alone.[4] No Icelandic artist – including Björk and Sigur Rós – has ever seen such swift success. The band has been touring the world since and their music has been featured in advertisements, television shows and films. Their sound and image does not emphasize Iceland in any way. Thus some fans have little knowledge about the band's place of origin.[5] The Icelandic card was never played in the promotion leading up to the debut's release, the band breaking America on their first attempt.[6]

OMAM also went against the grain in one very important manner: 'What's weird about us . . . ,' said Ragnar Þórhallsson, guitarist and singer, in an interview with *Morgunblaðið*, 'is that we are not weird!'[7] This off-the-cuff remark is in reality incredibly insightful as the 2010s saw Icelandic bands and artists swaying away from the well-trodden 'eccentric' path, as they entered the international stage. As a token of an ever more globalized world, these artists operate almost exclusively in the international market, using Iceland as a home base between tours.[8] This also begs the question: do Icelandic musicians

Of Monsters and Men (OMAM) cracked the U.S. pop market in spring 2012 and have enjoyed a successful career since.

who work (or make their living) outside of Iceland – whether as travelling rock, jazz or classical musicians, or writing soundtracks for films and advertisers – have a sense of themselves as Icelandic musicians? Is such an identity tied up with ways of working or with some sort of national sensibility? This is of particular interest now because of the way in which technological developments make it ever easier to be part of a music-making community that is not defined by the occupation of a shared national space.

Other acts comparable to OMAM this decade are Ásgeir and KALEO. Neither act accentuates their Icelandicness specifically. It has been subtly flagged but it's not the jumping-off point. For a long while, being different seemed to be the way out of the country (The Sugarcubes, Björk, Sigur Rós). But today, playing the quirky Icelandic card is no longer the only option if you want to get a footing in the international pop world.

The musical evolution story of Ásgeir is quite remarkable. He burst onto the scene in 2012, just shy of twenty years old and had been taken under the wing of Kiddi Hjálmur. Kiddi produced the debut album, the magnificent *Dýrð í dauðaþögn* (In the Silence), a work that is framed within a contemporary singer-songwriter style (think Bon Iver, for instance). The album garnered attention not least for how beautifully it unfolded and how effortlessly it flowed into the hearts of the Icelanders. Domestic sales now stand at 40,000 copies (8× platinum). Ásgeir would prove himself to be an explorative, vibrant artist, and *Afterglow* (2017) was distinctly more electronic and refreshingly different from the debut. The third studio album *Sátt/Bury the Moon* (2020) brought further changes; a more grounded and organic album, a sort of tender, heartfelt ode to the home country's landscapes.[9] It was his 'Iceland' album. Ásgeir tours the world regularly (he has a strong fan base in Australia, for instance) and has a solid international reputation.

KALEO, founded in 2012 in Mosfellsbær, competed in Músíktilraunir in 2013 and reached the finals but did not secure a winning

Ásgeir has garnered a global audience with his heartfelt, sincere music.

position. However, the band compensated for this setback by establishing itself as one of Iceland's most successful music exports. The music, a blend of bluesy rock with a stadium-friendly sound reminiscent of bands like Kings of Leon, gained momentum quickly. Their first breakthrough was a cover of the Icelandic classic 'Vor í Vaglaskógi', which received massive domestic airplay in 2013. Their eponymous debut album, released the same year, was well received in Iceland, paving the way for a successful European tour. In 2015 KALEO relocated to Austin after signing a deal with Atlantic Records in the USA. They embarked on a North American tour soon after and their music started appearing in American television shows; the song 'Way Down We Go' featured in an episode of NBC's *Blindspot*, eventually reaching over a billion streams on Spotify. Their album *A/B* (2016) peaked at number 16 on the Billboard 200 chart. Their third album, *Surface Sounds*, was finally released in early 2021 after some delays caused by the COVID-19 pandemic. The band has made frequent appearances on various U.S. late-night television shows and 'Way Down We Go' has been featured in popular U.S. TV series like *Grey's Anatomy*, *The Vampire Diaries* and *Riverdale*, as well as in video games such as *FIFA 16*, *NFL 17* and *NHL 18*. KALEO occupies a distinctive place in Icelandic music culture. Unlike OMAM and Ásgeir, who primarily focus on the international scene, KALEO's strong presence in the USA sets them apart. However, like OMAM, KALEO's origins can sometimes be ambiguous for listeners.

These three artists have emerged as the most notable foreign success stories this decade. In addition, Júníus Meyvant (Unnar Gísli Sigurmundsson) quickly garnered attention on the international stage with his indie soul sound, reminiscent of artists like Matthew E. White and Dan Auerbach.

The metal subgenre was also going places this decade, both domestically and abroad. But before we delve into that, let's look back at Icelandic hip-hop, as promised in the preceding chapter. Gísli Pálmi's unassuming, unruly appeal sparked a second wave of Icelandic hip-hop in 2015, and his self-titled debut album, released that year, remains a seminal work. We're still awaiting the follow-up. The preconditions of this second wave are completely different from those of the first wave. There is more diversity, and the scene is much more visible on the mainstream market, which is in line with developments abroad, where hip-hop has become the dominant genre, surpassing rock music in popularity.

At the time of writing, the scene as such has died down, but the most important players have merged with the mainstream, lightening their approach and aligning with the global takeover of hip-hop. While the first wave was all about macho gangs, the second wave of Icelandic hip-hop is much more varied. There are more solo artists, more women, more pop and R&B and more experimentation.

Emmsjé Gauti is the approachable nice guy that everyone loves while the duo Úlfur Úlfur (Wolf Wolf), hailing from the countryside, is the smart person's group. Reykjavíkurdætur (Daughters of Reykjavík) is a powerful political feminist hip-hop collective comprising a diverse group of women. Additionally, it's the only hip-hop group in the country to have an international standing of sorts. Sturla Atlas is a melodic, R&B-leaning rapper who performs in English. Aron Can introduced Icelandic emotional rap to the scene, influenced by Drake but also by trap artists such as Future and Young Thug. His music is stripped down and shadowy. Hr. Hnetusmjör (Mr. Peanut Butter) went for all-out capitalist venture rap, reminiscent of the great Rick Ross, while Lord Pusswhip squats in the noisy underground. These are just a few examples showcasing the diversity within the second wave of Icelandic hip-hop.

This time around women have made their mark, whereas they were almost invisible in the first wave. Along with Reykjavíkurdætur we have CYBER, Countess Malaise, Fever Dream and Alvia Islandia, who have released progressive and sometimes very surreal material that is at once gender-political and strange. The innovation that thrives in the second wave of Icelandic hip-hop even earned Alvia Islandia a well-deserved nomination for the Nordic Music Prize in 2018.[10]

The second wave managed to renew itself quickly in the early years and it peaked in the autumn of 2017 when JóiPé x Króli's song 'B.O.B.A.' became a huge hit. Smooth R&B also made its way into the mainstream with songstresses GDRN and BRÍET.

Now, let's talk metal. This decade witnessed the emergence of new metal scenes as well as the fortification of bands that had previously enjoyed success but went to even greater heights. We'll begin with Iceland's only active Viking-metal band (there should be more, right?), Skálmöld. The band's journey began innocently enough in 2009, with six friends mostly from the north coming together weekly to play heavy metal inspired by the likes of Iron Maiden. As they accumulated songs for a possible release, no Icelandic label showed interest. Instead, the courageous minds at the Faroese label Tutl, led by the venerable and wise Kristian Blak, took the leap and released their debut album *Baldur* in 2010. Featuring lyrics reminiscent of the old Eddas and a blend of thrashy, melodic metal, the album quickly gained popularity. With their image and artwork on point, coupled with the charismatic individuals in the group, Skálmöld could do no wrong. In 2011 they signed a contract with Napalm Records, catapulting the band to greater success.

Albums were now released at successive two-year intervals, followed by concert tours across Europe together with the establishment of fan clubs, band merchandise and other miscellaneous activities. The band members, mostly settled family men, were initially surprised by the rapid success but embraced it wholeheartedly (you can almost touch the obvious camaraderie between the members). The albums were, of course, firmly within the aesthetics of Viking metal, but the band tastefully and subtly pushed the boundaries from within with every album. As their career progressed, Skálmöld participated in three events that highlighted their Icelandic heritage somewhat. This was in the winter of 2013–14 and the first one was at an evening celebrating the life and work of manuscript collector and philologist Árni Magnússon, commemorating the 350th anniversary of his birth. This was at Iceland's National Theatre and attended by members of Iceland's cultural elite along with dignitaries such as the Queen of Denmark and the President of Iceland. The second event consisted of three consecutive nights at the end of November 2013, during which Skálmöld collaborated with the Iceland Symphony Orchestra and three choirs to present their music in Eldborg, the main hall in the Harpa concert hall (later released as an album). The final collaboration was a semi-theatrical live production of Skálmöld's debut album *Baldur*, staged and performed at Borgarleikhúsið, the city-operated theatre.[11]

Emphasizing their roots was never a deliberate intention of the band, and they were more or less just going along with the opportunities handed to them. However, the fact that this is a Viking metal band from Iceland certainly helped overseas. A German fan once proclaimed, 'Wow, a Viking band singing in the language of the

Vikings!'[12] The band maintains a loyal fan base, both domestically and internationally, and its journey is akin to a modern-day Cinderella story in many respects.[13]

Another band enjoying vindication in the 2010s was Sólstafir, a black metal band formed in 1995.[14] Today, it's the most well-known heavy/extreme metal band from Iceland, as evidenced by its Spotify streams, touring activity and headlining slots at festivals (for example, a tour with Paradise Lost across the USA in 2018). In the year the band was formed, a cassette titled *Í norðri* (In the North) was released. The music was in the style of frostbitten Norwegian black metal, which was all the rage at the time, although the rocking guitar tone hinted at what would unfold in the future. The melodic title track also served as evidence that this band was in it for the long haul. Soon enough, the band began to experiment, and their debut album, *Í blóði og anda* (In Blood and Spirit, 2002), featured songs that referenced Motörhead and Sonic Youth. The 'Black Death' 7-inch, released later that year, was infused with 'black 'n' roll', showcasing a band well aware of the image and spirit of Lemmy Kilmister, Motörhead's leader. The subsequent albums demonstrated a steady progression. *Masterpiece of Bitterness* was released in 2005 on the Finnish label Spikefarm, followed by *Köld* (Cold) in 2009. The music had now evolved beyond the confines of black metal and had become more gothic, with influences from bands like The Cure and The Sisters of Mercy.[15] An amazing promotional photo from this time shows the band resembling gothic spaghetti western cowboys transported to the Victorian age. Sólstafir began touring regularly around this time, and in 2011 *Svartir sandar* (Black Sands) was released. The journey away from black metal was now complete, the tag 'post-metal' fitting and shades of Sigur Rós's ethereal beauty were to be found. Long, epic songs characterize the album and the band ventured fearlessly into unknown territories.[16] French metal label giant Season of Mist released *Ótta* in 2014 and Sólstafir's career has remained steadfast in terms of brave musical adventures to this day.[17] Long-time fans sometimes ponder the question 'Is this metal?' while Sólstafir simply refuse to rest on their laurels and have reaped the benefits accordingly.

Dimma (Darkness) is the third band of considerable size that emerged this decade. Hometown heroes first and foremost, their straightforward heavy metal music evokes the spirits of Judas Priest and Dio, spiced up with a hefty dose of northern darkness. In 2011 the band experienced a rejuvenation when a new drummer (Birgir Jónsson) and singer (Stefán Jakobsson) joined the Geirdal brothers, who led the band. Dimma is an esteemed band in Icelandic heavy metal circles and also among mainstream audiences who enjoy rocking out.

The Vintage Caravan is, on the other hand, a curious example of a band that has enjoyed a successful career as a touring group on foreign soil, while their popularity in their home country is less pronounced. Their music is a blend of stoner/psychedelic rock with classic 1970s heavy metal thrown in. The band was formed in 2006 when the members were just twelve years old, and it quickly became evident that guitarist Óskar Logi Ágústsson was a prodigy. The band signed a contract with the renowned label Nuclear Blast in 2013, which subsequently released their second album *Voyage* internationally in 2014. The band has been actively touring since then, undertaking regular European tours and even travelling to South America.

In 2015, on my return to Iceland after spending three years in Scotland pursuing my Master's and PhD studies, I met up with D.G., the leader of the band Misþyrming (Maltreatment). He carried his band's debut album, *Söngvar elds og óreiðu* (Songs of Fire and Chaos). I was literally blown away when the first notes attacked me from the speakers, charging out of the gates like bloodthirsty gladiators. The album simply didn't let up after that, each song absolutely relentless. Grim, evil . . . mad. Beautiful, bonkers and absolutely brilliant. D.G. duly informed me that a new era was dawning in Icelandic black metal and the 2010s were to be that decade.

I had often wondered why black metal, which was so colourful and boundary-breaking in the 1990s and beyond, hadn't had more of an impact here. We never had a scene, just stray bands, and this subgenre thrives almost everywhere in the Nordic countries, except perhaps in Denmark. Iceland, with its landscape, darkness and cold, seems like the perfect host for such music. Nevertheless, it struggled to take root. We had powerful death metal and hardcore scenes, but black metal bands were few and far between. However, in 2015 things were indeed different. A massive surge had taken place in the black metal scene, with bands emerging around labels like Vánagandr, run by the Misþyrming clique. Bands like Svartidauði, Sinmara, Abominor, Dynfari, Zhrine, Wormlust and Naðra were all active at this time, each with its own unique style, ranging from harsh, rugged black metal to progressive and epic, with room for ambient/one-man metal as well.[18]

Come 2018 the scene was robust. Both the atmospheric faction, counting for example Sólstafir, Auðn, Katla and Zhrine, and the

Misþyrming have been at the forefront of a vibrant black metal scene since the release of their debut album in 2015.

brutal faction, Misþyrming and co., were making inroads. At that year's Roadburn Festival, representatives from the Icelandic scene performed a long piece under the title *Sól án varma* (Sun Without Radiance). Bands played shows all over Europe and also in the USA. Online merch sales were thriving as well and the Internet played a crucial role in facilitating connections, marketing, promotion and distribution of music, enabling Icelandic bands to establish a presence in the international extreme metal community. Opportunities that had been out of reach 25 years ago were seized. There is also an interesting Irish connection: one Stephen Lockhart (Rebirth of Nefast) is based in Mosfellsbær, where he runs Studio Emissary and has recorded a multitude of Icelandic black metal bands. He has also overseen the Ascension festival.[19]

Black metal activity has remained stable to this day. The band Vampíra won the 2024 edition of Músíktilraunir (the first black metal band to do so), and other extreme scenes, such as the death metal scene, are doing well even if they have had to endure some ups and downs over the years. Maintaining long-term stability in scenes, particularly as they gravitate towards niche genres, is challenging due to Iceland's small population.

Punk rock has always been a constant, but more as an outlier compared to the heavy metal culture. In this decade we saw high activity, but concentrated on a few bands, labels and venues. One mini-scene revolved around the label PBP (Paradísarborgarplötur, Paradise City Records) and bands like Börn (Children) and Dauðyflin (Lazy Bastards/Zombies). The music is generally released on Bandcamp but cassettes are a popular medium as well. It is often speedy anarcho-punk but there's also room for all kinds of underground music – dungeon synth and industrial-inspired post-punk, as seen in ROHT, for instance, led by couple Þórir Georg and Júlía Aradóttir. Þórir has been a constant presence in the Icelandic underground scene for the last 25 years or so and he has dozens of albums featuring a variety of bands and artist names under his belt, ranging from melodic emocore and folky singer-songwriter stuff to atmospheric black metal. Another important scene formed around the firesoul Ægir Sindri Bjarnason, who helms the Why Not? label. A drummer and a member of numerous bands (the beautiful grindcore band World Narcosis being one of many), he also runs the R6013 venue in downtown Reykjavík, a small place with an enormous heart. Started in 2017, it's still one of the most important hubs for underground concerts and general networking between the main underground scenesters.[20]

Before we leave this all-around heaviness, I must mention Kælan Mikla, a goth band that has been one of the more interesting Icelandic musical fairy tales of late. The band was founded in early 2013 by Sólveig Matthildur Kristjánsdóttir, Margrét Rósa Dóru-Harrysdóttir and Laufey Soffía Þórsdóttir. They met and formed the band when Sólveig participated in a poetry slam at Menntaskólinn við Hamrahlíð. The music draws from the 'darkwave' scene, enveloped in gloomy, gothic rock-like sounds with a strong reference to the early 1980s (like a Nordic variation of The Cure's *Faith* album).[21] The band went from strength to strength during this decade, quickly gaining fans worldwide, armed with an impressive work ethic and terrific imagery. The excitement around the band became so strong that The Cure's leader, Robert Smith himself, hand-picked the band to warm up for his band at a Hyde Park concert in 2018. Kælan's music has sharpened with each release, becoming more streamlined but more thought-out at the same time. It's simply better and more solid, forward-thinking in every way, even within the constraints of the punishing goth aesthetics.[22]

Another entity that established strong connections abroad this decade was Fufanu. The music is export-ready, goth-infused electropop, with both experimental flair and a melodic tinge. Vocalist Kaktus Einarsson has now forged a respectable solo career, his latest album, the alt-pop gem *Lobster Coda* (2024), making waves in the international press.

Sóley's dreamlike, ephemeral avant-pop flourished in the 2000s and earned her international acclaim.

One of the artists of the decade was the extraordinary Sóley. She started out in the Icelandic indie scene but broke through as a fully formed musician with a six-track EP, *Theater Island* (2010), which is a wonderfully atmospheric record, referencing Erik Satie and classical minimalism but always guided by heart-tugging, engaging melodicism: 'The atmosphere is thus a significant part of the work; it's dark yet innocent . . . solitary yet uplifting.'[23] More albums followed in a similar vein and would have an impact internationally, enabling Sóley to tour the world. Her output has been varied and alongside her 'formal' albums there have been records with pure experimental music (for example *Harmóník I* and *II*, 2017 and 2020, where drone music is the order of the day). *Mother Melancholia* (2021), her most recent studio album, was quite the departure from her previous offerings, in reality one long meditation on the state of the world, drifting between pretty and horrific. The music moves elegantly in distinctive parts, melding Sóley's experimental work with more harmonious, exquisite sections.[24]

Sóley began her musical journey in the band Seabear under the leadership of Sindri Már Sigfússon. Sindri embarked on a fruitful solo career in 2008 under the moniker Sin Fang Bous (later simplified to Sin Fang) and released his work throughout the decade on Morr Music, like múm and Sóley. His music can be described as eccentric indie pop, following the same blueprint that put Iceland on the map for international music enthusiasts, drawing from the legacy of Björk. Sin Fang's albums are known for their dense, pulsating electro-pop sound with hints of psychedelia, featuring layered compositions that sometimes give the impression of multiple songs playing simultaneously, skilfully balancing accessibility and experimentation.[25] Of a similar stature is Ólöf Arnalds. In 2007 she released *Við og við* (Us and Us, but also Every Now and Then). The album was released on the 12 Tónar record label and was subsequently released in the USA and the UK after she signed with One Little Independent Records in 2009. A magnificent debut album, with beautiful, heartfelt and ever-so-folky songs, it travelled widely, and its success in the USA led to Ólöf touring with artists such as Blonde Redhead, Björk and Jeff Mangum (Neutral Milk Hotel). Ólöf's second album, *Innundir Skinni* (Under the Skin), was released in 2010, produced by Sigur Rós member Kjartan Sveinsson and Davíð Þór Jónsson, and featuring contributions from Björk, Skúli Sverrisson, Shahzad Ismaily and María Huld Markan Sigfúsdóttir.[26] Her third album, *Sudden Elevation*, was sung entirely in English.

Naturally, this decade also had its fair share of mainstream domestic music. It's not just about catering to the hipsters. Three bands have been at the forefront, enjoying popularity with the Icelandic masses. Moses Hightower play jazz-led pop music, quite accessible but oddly strange at the same time, giving it both substance and appeal.[27] Another group to come from Keflavík is Valdimar, a distinctly Icelandic band that stepped into an age-old legion of bands that are more 'domestic' than 'foreign'. Their albums are all cohesive works, containing refined indie pop-rock that evokes bands like Elbow and Hjaltalín.[28] Dikta had released two albums in the 2000s, but it was their third album, released at the end of the decade, that finally shot them to stardom. While momentum had been building, *Get It Together* (2009) was the breakthrough that solidified their success. Dikta's music had evolved from garage grunge into accessible pop/rock, reminiscent of Coldplay and Leaves, with gentle melodies interspersed with powerful, noisy bursts. Tracks from the album received considerable airplay and the album was marketed in Germany, Austria and Switzerland. This success led to an extensive European tour and a UK tour with The Kooks in 2010. The band was active for another half a decade but faded from view after the album *Easy Street* (2015).[29]

Prins Póló (Svavar Pétur Eysteinsson) was one of Iceland's most fascinating popular music icons. He named himself after a Polish chocolate bar that is very popular here, the everyman's favourite, if you will. As an artist name, it neatly embodies the everyday magic that Svavar was prone to infuse into his art. He reached the masses in the later stages of his career without shedding an ounce of his artistic integrity. 'The Prince', as he was often affectionately called, was a multifaceted artist, working in music, graphic design, fine art and clothing, and also branching out into food manufacturing (vegan sausages and crisps). Eventually, he became a farmer in the Eastfjords – alongside all these activities – and quickly transformed the farmstead into a cultural centre.

Musically, he started out in indie bands in the 1990s but later developed his solo alter ego, Prins Póló. As such, he released albums in the 2010s, culminating in the wonderful *Þriðja kryddið* (The Third Spice, 2018). His style could be described as quirky singer-songwriter music with an indie twist, but as his career progressed, he started to simplify things and in a way made his music deliberately more crass.

Prins Póló (Svavar Pétur Eysteinsson) adorns the cover of his brilliant album *Þriðja kryddið* (The Third Spice, 2018).

Interestingly, this only boosted his popularity, allowing his charm and sincerity to resonate with a wider audience. On *Þriðja kryddið* the music is stripped back. Simple computer beats and crude, box-shaped synthetic sounds from the 1990s. Kraftwerk in 'pocket' form. Melodies, but always unexpected twists and turns. In a review for RÚV, titled 'The Unbearable Lightness of Being', I wrote:

> The Third Spice is essentially a long contemplation on life and what it offers. The whole gallery, so to speak; fun and joy but also sorrow and heaviness. The self-reflection is absolute and

> 'The Prince' does this in an unusually sensitive way, keeping things meticulously balanced throughout the album.[30]

Originality mixed with accessibility. Glee and melancholia. Yin and yang. That was Svavar Pétur Eysteinsson's career. His untimely passing from cancer in September 2022 at the age of 45 was a huge loss for the Icelandic music community, reminiscent of the impact felt when young Fróði Finnsson passed away in 1994 at nineteen, also from cancer. Fróði had played a pivotal role in the vibrant death metal scene at the time (as a member of Sororicide) and in other scenes (SSSpan). It was evident that Fróði would have left a lasting impression on Icelandic music culture, much like Svavar, had he been given more time.[31]

Regarding the framework of the Icelandic popular music industry, there were various developments this decade. Institutionally, the opening of Harpa in 2011 – Iceland's first purpose-built concert hall – was incredibly important. Lobbying for a venue like this had been going on for decades – since 1930 to be exact, the year of the first Icelandic music boom. Harpa stands in Reykjavík's harbour, an architectural wonder dominating the surrounding scenery. In the very beginning, there was a tug of war between those who foresaw the building as a classical music venue first and foremost and those who wanted to have more fluidity between genres (the latter group 'won'). A huge venue ('like something from a foreign country' as one Icelander quipped), with room for everyone, thanks to the relatively small Icelandic music scene.[32]

Reykjavík in the mid-2010s: there are big buildings on the seafront to the east near the city centre and Harpa. They suggest skyscrapers, but they are still too small and 'cute'. Reykjavík is getting bigger; the capital area numbered 240,000 people in 2022 and today you can drive past neighbourhoods you didn't know existed when you run a surprise errand in the east side of the city. The demography is also changing. Of Iceland's inhabitants, 5.8 per cent are

Polish (over 20,000 people) but you don't see this at all in the music culture. Class divisions in Iceland are for the first time very clear and we are as corrupt as the big nations we dream of emulating. We are getting more modern in so many ways, while we are still unsure what we want to be when we grow up.

An artist collective, post-dreifing, was formed in this decade (2017). It would go on to have a huge effect on the Icelandic underground scene – we have to go all the way back to Bad Taste to find comparable activity and influence. The collective consisted of people in their teens, some in their early twenties, operating on very level premises, with no specific spokesperson for the community. Inspired by anarcho-philosophies and anti-capitalism, all decisions were made at informal meetings with no one having more power than the next person. The primary contribution of this Generation Z-led gang to Icelandic music culture has been their overall activity: initiating projects and keeping them vibrant. The motto 'do it together' (DIT) is held in high regard, advancing the 'do it yourself' ethos (DIY).[33] What can be accomplished with the power of the masses has indeed been particularly visible: a multitude of concerts, releases and so on, by various bands and artists; and the group's ideology, whether it's in politics, aesthetic emphasis or environmental and gender issues, colours everything.[34] As it stands, post-dreifing's current activity may not be as intense as it was, but its impact is deeply felt by a new generation of creative, underground musicians.[35]

The opening of the Mengi venue in 2013 was an important event, establishing a permanent space where the Icelandic underground scene could come together and evolve. It's situated, like so many places mentioned in this respect, in downtown Reykjavík, highlighting 'Reykjavík's compact spatial configuration' in terms of cultural activities, most hubs being a block or three away from each other.[36] For the younger participants, the venue feels like a sort of experimental music nursery school.[37] There's a busy schedule every

Mengi was opened in 2013 and caters to new and experimental music, made by Icelandic and international artists. It lies in the heart of the Þingholt neighbourhood, near downtown Reykjavík.

week, frequently featuring visits by innovative left-field artists from abroad, sparking a vibrant exchange of ideas in both directions.

Let's wrap up this chapter with some glamorous fireworks. Well, mostly. Eurovision is a big deal in Iceland. It's a social event that brings families and friends together every year. People gather around the television set with snacks and BBQ food and debate over the second verse in Estonia's song. The competition can be highly political, both musically and externally. In 2024 we witnessed a clear example of this, where some countries threatened to withdraw on the day of the finals due to Israel's military operations in Gaza. In 2019, when the competition took place in Tel Aviv, a band from Iceland, Hatari (Hater), competed as Iceland's entry. Their music is industrial techno-rock with a public image that incorporates elements of anti-capitalism and BDSM attire. Their act was a mix of performance art and political messaging, and prior to the contest, the band had attracted attention for their political statements regarding the Israeli presence in Palestine. Despite a warning from the European Broadcasting Union (EBU), after Iceland's televote score was announced during the final, Hatari members unveiled a banner featuring the Palestinian flag.[38]

Following the competition, Hatari were active, touring Europe, but things quieted down as the pandemic emerged. Lastly, as a new decade began, a Hollywood film titled *Eurovision Song Contest: The Story of Fire Saga* premiered in the summer of 2020. Starring Will Ferrell and directed by Dave Dobkin, the film humorously parodies the song competition, telling the tale of Icelanders from Húsavík who dream of winning it. The film had some small tourism benefits but overall Icelanders mostly shrugged it off with a half-smile.[39]

Laufey's post-war jazz pop has catapulted her to global stardom in record time. Here she performs at La Madeleine in Brussels, Belgium, 21 February 2024.

8

The 2020s: Where to Next?

During the summer of 2021, I actively searched for a female artist to feature as the 'Record of the Week' on RÚV (its guidelines emphasize maintaining a diverse selection of music throughout the year, as mandated by equality principles). I stumbled upon a seven-song record, *Typical of Me*, by an artist named Laufey, whom I knew nothing about. But her music was pleasant enough and radio-friendly and I included her in my notes. Little did I know that she would become the biggest music news in Iceland since Björk.

A classically trained musician, Laufey graduated from the prestigious Berklee College of Music and now lives in Los Angeles, the entertainment capital of the world. Her career has been nothing short of amazing. At the time of writing, spring 2024, she is the most streamed Icelandic artist on Spotify, her concerts sell out within minutes and she has been featured on the covers of *Billboard*, NME, *Eurowoman* and *Female*, as well as countless online publications. She has appeared on both traditional media (she hosted a radio show for the BBC and has been featured on popular talk shows) and new media (she collaborated with Beabadoobee on TikTok and performed on NPR's Tiny Desk Concert series). She released a Christmas single with Norah Jones in December 2023 and after accepting a Grammy in 2024 for the Best Traditional Pop Vocal Album she stayed on the stage to play cello – with Billy Joel! Laufey is equally at home in a ball gown with a symphony orchestra or uploading content on social media and can carry both activities with aplomb. Laufey and her team have mastered the art of appealing to both mainstream and niche audiences and she builds bridges between older people who appreciate classical music and younger people who prefer electronic music. She seamlessly moves between different platforms, generations and genres, reflecting the way that people consume media in the twenty-first century.

Laufey has been credited with making post-war jazz popular with young people but her success is ultimately due to her musical abilities. Her unique voice transcends time, combining jazz with a modern pop sensibility. Her singing voice is beautiful, deep and enveloping, with the experience and maturity of a much older singer. Her sound is reminiscent of her singing heroes: Ella Fitzgerald, Billie Holiday and Chet Baker. The only thing missing from her music is the crackling sound of a 78 RPM record.

This was the major news of the decade, and Icelanders are still coming to terms with it. In many ways, this decade is progressing as the women's decade. The biggest domestic pop stars have been soulstress GDRN, pop diva BRÍET, the confessional Una Torfa and Elín Hall, singer-songwriter Árný Margrét and electro-pop musician gugusar. Despite this trend, women have, of course, been grossly under-represented in Iceland's popular music history, reflecting the sad, stale state of the industry's prevalent male-dominated culture at large. In recent years, efforts from the industry and grassroots associations have slowly improved gender balance in Icelandic music. Músíktilraunir has encouraged more women and non-binary individuals to participate, with recent winners being either female or female-fronted groups. Initiatives like Læti! / Stelpur rokka! (Loud! / Girls Rock!) and the founding of KÍTÓN (Organization of Icelandic Women in Music) in 2013 have also contributed to this progress, and juries, music boards, radio personnel and critics have become increasingly aware of the gender gap in music representation.

GDRN, real name Guðrún Ýr Eyfjörð Jóhannesdóttir, is one of Iceland's most prominent pop stars at the time of writing.

This atmosphere has in turn encouraged women to release their stuff and we've seen a lot of albums and EPS by relative unknowns uploaded to streaming sites in the last few years. And the music is of all kinds: Nordic noir-infused R&B, singer-songwriter material, epic divadom and straight-up electronic pop. We see trail-blazing women like producer/songwriter/singer Hildur and singer/actress and radio personality par excellence Salka Sól. We also see the female trio GRÓA, by far the most exciting band to come out of post-dreifing; we watch JFDR conjure magic and mystery in her dreamlike music, as do MSEA, dj. flugvél og geimskip and the twin sisters from múm, Kristín Anna and Gyða, their respective solo careers awe-inspiring spectacles

(Gyða was awarded the Nordic Council Music Prize in 2019 for her artistry). Asalaus (Ása Önnu Ólafsdóttir) is our one to watch at the moment, and I have to mention Bára Gísladóttir, our supernova at the time of writing, seamlessly orchestrating noise-art, drone, avant-jazz, classical music and 'outer limits' adventures.

Singer Elly Vilhjálms was mentioned in the 1970s chapter. She had a rich career in the 1960s and '70s and enjoyed immense popularity. She lived a colourful life and in 2017 a play about her debuted at Borgarleikhúsið. The play broke the theatre's attendance records and ended its first run in 2019 after 220 shows (it had a short second run in 2024–5). It's not obvious why this particular play became so popular but Elly, like all women in the popular music industry, had to swim against the tide. As did the giants who followed in her footsteps from the 1980s onwards: Helga Möller, one half of the legendary disco duet Þú og ég and a songstress in her own right; Ellen Kristjánsdóttir, the soothing siren of Mannakorn and later a solo artist (and her three daughters sing together in Systur (Sisters)); Andrea Gylfadóttir, Guðrún Gunnarsdóttir and Ragnhildur Gísladóttir, aka Ragga, with her captivating presence. Later, musicians like Lára Rúnarsdóttir and Ragnheiður Gröndal would launch successful careers, releasing album after album of quality material.[1] *Vögguvísur* (Lullabies) by Hafdís Huld of GusGus fame is the most streamed album in Icelandic history, the eternally cool Svala is just one of many pristine pop queens we've managed to foster, and Vök travels Europe and America with the immaculate Margrét Rán out in front. I could go on. These are broad strokes, but we need to name names in order to see and understand that this part of the music culture exists; it's vibrant, it matters and it has a lineage, often downtrodden by the (male) powers that be. But we see them now. And hear them.

The other big news from the world of export is Daði Freyr, he of Eurovision fame. He competed in the main competition in 2021 (postponed from 2020 because of COVID-19) and created a stir with his nerdcore technopop, where joviality prevailed in both the music and stage performance. Daði Freyr has travelled the world since and keeps a steady presence as a concert draw. Domestically, a fertile experimental (and sometimes not-so-experimental) jazz scene made itself heard, manned by an up-and-coming, young generation. Reykjavík Record Shop has released heaps of records by these musicians, keeping the scene alive. The music, which bridges worlds, is not straight-up jazz, rather an avant-garde one, drawing from noise-art, improv and liberal pop/rock strands. This scene, quite active in the last five years, has seen Krautrock-inspired melodicism and strangeness (Hist og, Ingibjörg Turchi), full-on noise madness (Tumi Árnason, Óskar Kjartansson) and something in between (Magnús Trygvason Eliassen, Tómas Jónsson, Óskar Guðjónsson, the prodigious Kári Egilsson and more).

Bass player Skúli Sverrisson, the grand magus of Icelandic avant-jazz and improv music, and a curator at Mengi (alongside Guðmundur Ari Arnalds, one of the most active underground musicians today) is a hovering presence in this music scene and occasionally contributes to its records. Skúli is a composer and multi-instrumentalist and

Daði Freyr's knowing wit and well-thought-out shenanigans made him a Eurovision favourite. Here he is with his band Gagnamagnið (The Data Plan).

was a key figure in the renowned downtown scene of New York in the 1990s. He has built a unique international career and has collaborated with a very broad spectrum of artists from the pop, jazz and classical world.[2]

We also have major 'general' contributors working in the Icelandic music scene at large, people that wear many hats, all-rounders like Magnús Jóhann, musician, producer and arranger, and Albert Finnbogason, producer par excellence. Behind the desk but in front of all things happening, if you will.

Logistically, we have not been able to cover the whole careers of all the musicians in the book. But pillars like Björk, Bubbi and Sigur Rós prevail. In the 2000s Björk would go on to release ever more adventurous albums, culminating in the grand project *Biophilia*, an app, instrument experiment, album and educational project, all in one. Her latest albums have been ambitious, ever original but first and foremost totally Björkian. Bubbi Morthens continues his journey unabated and in 2020 a musical about his life, *Níu líf* (Nine Lives), was premiered at Borgarleikhúsið. It ended its run on 15 June 2024 after 250 shows, a phenomenal success, with the audience numbering around 130,000. Sigur Rós remain an active band and after a ten-year studio album hiatus, they released a new album, *8*, in 2023. The fan base was kept busy in the interim with tours, reissues, solo endeavours, collaborations and special projects.

There are genres and subgenres that I have only touched upon here and some that I have not covered at all – 'Outsider' music, for instance, which will need its own book.[3] The scope of the book allows only for broad outlines. Where to next indeed?

Conclusion: Why Iceland?

> So, does Iceland 'punch above its weight' musically? That, of course, depends on who the comparators are, what a punch would look like in a musical context, and what weight we assume it should be punching at. In many respects, it is an attractive though diversionary question. Iceland's reputation is certainly surprising given its size, and much of this is down to how musicians and musical networks form on the island.

Thus asks Nick Prior in the conclusion of his article about music practices in Iceland.[1] What's interesting about the music from this European micronation? Are we as good as or even better than other nations when it comes to all things musical? Sometimes I get so childishly excited by these exclamations from foreigners that I'm prone to throw my academic hat out of the window and just go with it. Yes, we are better! And to turn to the Introduction again, how do we 'explain the phenomenon'? Is there something special going on in Iceland music-wise, really? And what are the peculiarities of the Icelandic popular music world compared to other worlds? What are the realities that set it apart from similar entities?

We have had good music through the decades, that's all very well, but the answer to the above lies in the social structure of the country. The small size of Icelandic society is a defining factor, directly influencing the workings of the popular music world where a 'village' factor is a determining dynamic in terms of communication, self-awareness, hopes and aspirations. The village is simultaneously strengthening and suffocating. The shared reality of the musicians, that is, being aware of the small market they are operating in, instills them with a pragmatic outlook, knowing that if they are determined to make a living out of music in Iceland, the chances of doing it squarely on their own terms are slim (working abroad is a separate thing).

If you are fairly open-minded, musically, you get to play styles that you maybe would never have a chance to encounter in a bigger society. Openness, versatility and a certain degree of cunningness will probably get you far in that situation. Cooperation in the village is therefore much in evidence, and a spirit of solidarity in the Icelandic pop/rock community is often mentioned in the foreign media, often dressed up in exaggerated language. But it's also true.[2] There is also a noticeable optimism regarding music-making in Iceland, which can be linked directly to the paragraph above. The easy access to media outlets for up-and-coming musicians and the general 'no-nonsense' air surrounding the popular music world, born out of the village factor, lends support to relatively high activity.

On the other side of the coin is the suffocating factor. Musicians interviewed for this author's PhD went so far as to talk about being locked in the village, where there was little variety in music, always the same people, lack of fresh ideas and so on. This is the dark side of the Icelandic music community. It's nigh on impossible to delve into any one thing. You could make a living off playing only avant-garde jazz in New York but not in Reykjavík. There was also a sense that everything was in one big heap, the inevitable overlap of different scenes and cultures a hindrance rather than a positive. In New York you can live and operate within a specific music culture and keep away from the mainstream culture. In Iceland, scenes, strands and worlds rub off each other constantly and the village does not offer any escape from its prevailing, mainstream culture. The population size, together with the close proximity, sees to that.

It's important to look at the nature of scenes in Icelandic music culture. Talk about an 'Icelandic scene' or 'Reykjavík scene' is misleading, as those scenes are not really recognized locally. The Reykjavík scene and the talk about all the exciting new music coming from Iceland usually refers to indie artists and left-field electronica acts that sometimes cater to what foreign media and scholars seek to find in Icelandic music. The template was laid by influential bands and artists in the 1990s and 2000s, and the musicians who have followed that design (consciously or not) have benefited in terms of press attention at the very least. The scenes that are not as interesting to international ears are more stable. We've had a pretty constant extreme metal scene since the late 1980s, which takes on various guises – it rises and falls, but is always present in some form. At the same time, Iceland is such a small country that some scenes just cannot be sustained. We had an alt-country scene that was in good health around 2002–5 but has not been seen or heard of since. By contrast, there is an ongoing alt-country scene in the UK and it's not going anywhere, made possible because of a population large enough to preserve it. All of the scenes that I've mentioned in this book are also quite fluid and you will often find a heavy metal drummer and an electronica DJ playing in a band that also features indie rockers. The small population and the micro-scenes that operate within thus force people to keep their hearts and minds open. Proximity is key here, the overlapping of different musicians, simple and easy communication lines, lack of bureaucracy and so on are all things that enable the relatively high activity detailed in the book, enriching a soil that helps the small music community to grow and thrive.

When legendary socio-musicologist Simon Frith visited Iceland in 2017, engaging with this author in a Q&A session in front of a packed auditorium at the University of Iceland, he remarked, and I am paraphrasing: 'When you have little or no chance of "making it" through the channels that are available in larger countries, that "non"-pressure enables you to do whatever you want in terms of music-making.' Frith continued to riff on this, that this freeing-up made for more relaxed, more risky music-making, as people literally had no expectations.[3] This is indeed true in the case of the early popular musicians here; OMAM of course step into a more tried-and-tested environment but they act on a cue, given to them by fellow countrymen. The music community here is intrinsic and close, for better or worse. To quote anthropologist Ruth Finnegan from her exquisite investigation into the music culture of English new town Milton Keynes: 'Settings in which relationships could be forged, interests shared, and a continuity of meaning achieved in the context of urban living. These pathways did more than provide the established routines of musical practice which people could choose to follow: they also had *symbolic depth*.'[4] These 'drivers' are among the defining factors of the Icelandic pop/rock community, along with the dynamics of Icelandic society at large, its customs and values. The musicians are engulfed by norms and conventions, particular to Icelandic society, enabling them to partake in the 'phenomenon' almost without realizing it.

References

Preface

1 Nick Prior, '"It's A Social Thing, Not a Nature Thing": Popular Music Practices in Reykjavík, Iceland', *Cultural Sociology*, IX/1 (2015), pp. 81–98 (p. 81).

2 The numbers game, that is, 'per capita', is played a lot in Iceland, especially when we need a shot of confidence regarding comparisons to other nations.

3 I once watched a quite esteemed academic, interested in Iceland and its music, roll out cliché after cliché and 'imagined truths' at a conference lecture without flinching.

4 Prior, 'It's A Social Thing', p. 81.

5 See Arnar Eggert Thoroddsen, 'Music-Making in a Northern Isle: Iceland and the "Village" Factor', PhD thesis, University of Edinburgh, 2019.

6 'Borealism' is a concept formulated by Icelandic ethnologist and folklorist Kristinn Schram that deals with exotic performances and representations of Icelanders and 'the North'. Found in, for example, Kristinn Schram, 'Banking on Borealism: Eating, Smelling, and Performing the North', in *Iceland and Images of the North*, ed. Daniel Chartier and Sumarliði R. Ísleifsson (Québec City, 2011), pp. 305–28.

7 See Kimberly Cannady, 'Echoes of the Colonial Past in Discourse on North Atlantic Popular Music', in *The Oxford Handbook of Popular Music in the Nordic Countries*, ed. Fabian Holt and Antti-Ville Kärjä (New York, 2017), pp. 203–18.

8 *Áfram með smjörið* means 'let's get on with it'. The literal meaning is 'on with the butter'.

Introduction: Music in Iceland, from the Beginning to the Popular Music Age

1 The exact year is disputed, but this is the one most referred to. The first settler – a rich Norwegian farmer – took land in Reykjavík, now the capital of Iceland. *Aðalstræti*, meaning Main Street, is the oldest street in Reykjavík, originally serving as the footpath to his farm. A transparent, small society indeed; Jón Þórarinsson's *Íslensk tónlistarsaga 1000–1800* (The History of Icelandic Music, 1000–1800) (Reykjavík, 2012) gives a detailed overview as does Baldur Andrésson's *Tónlistarsaga Reykjavíkur* (Reykjavík's Music History) (Reykjavík, 2008) which goes all the way back to the settlement era. Both works are available online but in Icelandic only. Also *Tónmenntasaga Íslands* by Hallgrímur Helgason (translates loosely as 'Iceland's Musical Literature') (Reykjavík, 1992). A fine BA thesis by Berglind Gestsdóttir on music life in Iceland in the twentieth century also contains good and succinct chapters on early music life: 'Hér er ekki leyfður grallarasöngur!: Helstu einkenni íslenskrar tónlistarmenningar á tímabilinu 1900–1930' (We Don't Allow the Old-Style Psalm Singing Here! The Main Characteristics of Icelandic Music Culture, 1900–1930), BA thesis, University of Iceland, 2014. I'm aware of the limitations of an undergraduate thesis as a source but as scholarly writing about this topic is slim, it is worth including here. I refer to additional similar theses in this book for the same reason. No general overview is available in English, although academic articles and essays on specific areas are out there and accumulating. The Icelandic scholars Árni Heimir Ingólfsson and Bjarki Sveinbjörnsson have been prolific in these matters. See also https://skemman.is, a digital repository for the universities of Iceland, containing students' final theses as well as scholarly research by the universities' academic staff until 2016.

2 See Baldur Andrésson in the aforementioned *Reykjavík's Music History*, and also Bjarni Þorsteinsson and his monumental work *Íslensk þjóðlög* (Icelandic Folk Songs) (Copenhagen, 1906–9), pp. 764–75. Árni Heimir's PhD from Harvard University has *tvísöngur* as a subject: 'These are the Things You Never Forget: The Written and Oral Traditions of Icelandic *Tvísöngur*', 2003.

3 People's first names, rather than surnames, are generally used in Iceland, both formally and informally. We will stick to that rule in this book. Viðar Hreinsson, *Bjarni Þorsteinsson – Eldhugi*

við ysta haf (Bjarni Þorsteinsson – A Pioneer in the World's Periphery) (Reykjavík, 2011), p. 61.

4 Berglind Gestsdóttir, 'We Don't Allow the Old-Style Psalm Singing Here!', p. 16.

5 See 'Hefðin og arfurinn – skilgreiningar' (The Tradition and the Heritage – Some Definitions), Kvæðamannafélagið Iðunn (Society for Traditional Icelandic Rimur – Chants and Intonation), www.rimur.is, accessed 21 January 2025.

6 Njáll Sigurðsson, 'Kveðskaparlistin: Varðveisla og saga' (The Art of Rhyme-Singing: Preservation and History), in *Silfurplötur Iðunnar* (The Silver Discs of Iðunn), ed. Gunnsteinn Ólafsson (Reykjavík, 2004), pp. 21–4. *The Silver Discs of Iðunn* is a record/book containing Icelandic rhymes and rhyme-singing.

7 Iðunn is a goddess in Norse mythology, associated with youth and rejuvenation.

8 A self-released six-track CD-R featuring Sigur Rós and Steindór was sold at the gigs – a rare item today.

9 David G. Woods, 'Íslenska langspilið' (The Icelandic Langspil), in *Árbók Hins íslenzka Fornleifafélags* (The Yearbook of the Icelandic Archaeological Association) (Reykjavík, 1994), pp. 109–28.

10 See Icelandic folk musicians Bára Grímsdóttir and Chris Foster's website for more information (www.funi-iceland.com).

11 A habitable cave in the south of Iceland, with some woodworks, was not abandoned until 1921. See 'Iceland's Cave People', *Iceland Monitor*, https://icelandmonitor.mbl.is, 18 April 2017.

12 Baldur Andrésson, *Reykjavík's Music History*.

13 This idiom refers to a person that 'burns' for a cause and makes certain sacrifices for it; Berglind Gestsdóttir, 'We Don't Allow the Old-Style Psalm Singing Here!', p. 27.

14 Baldur Andrésson, *Reykjavík's Music History*.

15 Ibid.

16 Hjálmar H. Ragnarsson, 'Jón Leifs', *Andvari – Tímarit Hins íslenska þjóðvinafélags og Bókaútgáfu Menningarsjóðs* (Andvari – Journal of the Icelandic Patriotic Society and the Cultural Fund's Publishing House), CXV/1 (1990), pp. 5–38. See also Árni Heimir Ingólfsson, *Jón Leifs and the Musical Invention of Iceland* (Bloomington, IN, 2019).

17 Baldur Andrésson, *Reykjavík's Music History*.

18 Helgi Jónsson, 'Pétur Á. Jónsson (1884–1956)', *Glatkistan*, www.glatkistan.com, 26 May 2016. Glatkistan is an impressive Icelandic music archive, edited by Helgi Jónsson. *Glatkista* translates

to 'vanishing box', suggesting that items placed inside it are lost, something the editor is trying to prevent.

19 Pétur was the first Icelander to sing on a record. It was released in 1910 but recorded in 1907 in Copenhagen as a single-sided 10-inch 78 RPM record.

20 Bjarki Sveinbjörnsson, 'Tónlistin á Íslandi: með sérstakri áherslu á upphaf og þróun elektrónískrar tónlistar á árunum 1960–90' (The Music in Iceland: With Special Emphasis on the Origins and Developments of Electronic Music, 1960–90), PhD thesis, Aalborg University, 1997. The thesis gives a great overview of Icelandic music in the first half of the twentieth century. Available at www.musik.is ('Tónlist á Íslandi á 20. öld' under 'Sérvefir').

1 The 1950s: Rock from the Base

1 See 'Lýðveldiskosningarnar', *Morgunblaðið*, 25 May 1944 and *Lýðveldishátíðin* (Reykjavík, 1945) (both authors anonymous). *Lýðveldi* means democracy. The first reference is an article about the election and the second is a book about the independence festivities.

2 Egill Helgason, 'Iceland and the Rest of the World', *Reykjavík Grapevine*, https://grapevine.is, 10 May 2012.

3 Matthew Campbell, 'Crossing the Concertina Wire: Icelandic-American Pop-Performance Relations On and Off Keflavik Naval Base During the Cold War', paper presented at the Music and Diplomacy conference, Tufts University, 1 March 2013.

4 Dr. Gunni (Gunnar Lárus Hjálmarsson), assisted by Haukur S. Magnússon, *Blue Eyed Pop: The History of Popular Music in Iceland* (Reykjavík, 2013), p. 28.

5 Ibid., p. 33.

6 Ibid.

7 Gestur Guðmundsson, *Rokksaga Íslands: frá Sigga Johnnie til Sykurmolanna* (Iceland's Rock History: From Siggi Johnnie to The Sugarcubes) (Reykjavík, 1990), p. 33.

8 Ibid.

9 Ásgeir Jónsson, *Why Iceland? How One of the World's Smallest Countries Became the Meltdown's Biggest Casualty* (New York, 2009), p. 10.

10 Gestur Guðmundsson, *Iceland's Rock History*, p. 28.

11 Dr. Gunni, *Stuð vors lands: Saga dægurtónlistar á Íslandi* (One Jovial Nation: Iceland's Popular Music History) (Reykjavík, 2012), p. 83.

12 Dr. Gunni, *Blue Eyed Pop*, p. 32.

13 Ibid., p. 33.

14 Ibid., p. 33; and Jónatan Garðarsson, *Erla Þorsteinsdóttir – Stúlkan með lævirkjaröddina* (2000), CD liner notes.
15 The records, along with detailed information and sleeve scans, can be obtained at the Discogs database (www.discogs.com), as is the case with most of the artists and records detailed in the book.
16 Eggert Þór Bernharðsson, *Undir bárujárnsboga: Braggalíf í Reykjavík 1940–1970* (Under an Iron Bow: Barrack-Living in Reykjavík, 1940–1970) (Reykjavík, 2000).

2 The 1960s: We Got the Beat (as Well)

1 See 'Lífið á Vellinum – bók um samskipti heimamanna og Varnarliðsmnna [sic]', *Víkurfréttir*, www.vf.is, 20 December 2020.
2 Dr. Gunni (Gunnar Lárus Hjálmarsson), assisted by Haukur S. Magnússon, *Blue Eyed Pop: The History of Popular Music in Iceland* (Reykjavík, 2013), p. 40.
3 Reissue giant Ace Records in the UK released a nice compilation album in 2001 titled *From Keflavík,... with love.*
4 The *sveitaball* or 'country dance' is an intrinsic, Icelandic phenomenon, deeply ingrained in the rural areas of the country. There's a quite detailed and insightful BA thesis on the topic available in Icelandic, written in the field of folklore/ethnography: Rebekka Blöndal, 'Þar sem ægir saman alls kyns lýð í erg og gríð: Sveitaböll fyrr og síðar' (Where There's Shoddy Shenanigans and All Kinds of Rabble Rousers – Country Dances Then and Now), BA thesis, University of Iceland, 2013.
5 Sæbjörn Valdimarsson, 'Keflvíska poppbyltingin', *Morgunblaðið*, 19 April 2005, p. 46.
6 Gestur Guðmundsson, *Rokksaga Íslands: frá Sigga Johnnie til Sykurmolanna* (Iceland's Rock History: From Siggi Johnnie to The Sugarcubes) (Reykjavík, 1990), p. 93.
7 Beat groups naturally sprang up all around the country in this decade, modelling themselves after The Beatles. Such local bands served their rural communities by playing the country dances, often operating for decades. Styles of music went in and out of fashion but people's need for entertainment and to dance their troubles away did not. Many names are lost to the mists of time but Mánar (The Moons) from South Iceland deserve a mention. They even managed a full LP in 1971, an eponymous one released by SG-Records, a record that enjoys a cult status today.
8 Dr. Gunni, *Blue Eyed Pop*, p. 46.
9 Ibid.

10 Ibid.
11 Gestur Guðmundsson, *Iceland's Rock History*, p. 97.
12 Savanna Trio, *Folksongs from Iceland* (1964), liner notes.
13 Jónatan Garðarsson, 'Savanna Tríóið', *ÍSMÚS* (*Íslenskur Músík & Menningararfur* (Icelandic Music and Cultural Heritage)), www.ismus.is, accessed 1 October 2024. Jónatan's writing was originally published on the *Land og Saga* (Land and History) website (www.landogsaga.is), the occasion being a grand reissue of all the Savanna Trio recordings.
14 Arnar Eggert Thoroddsen, 'Góða veislu gjöra skal', *Morgunblaðið*, 20 December 2009, pp. 36–7.
15 After the mid-1970s, Þórir found himself in Munich, working alongside Giorgio Moroder (as Thor Baldursson) on albums by Donna Summer, Grace Jones and Elton John.
16 Gestur Guðmundsson, *Iceland's Rock History*, p. 122.

3 The 1970s: Folkloric Prog and Socio-Realistic Pop

1 The one exception is Eik, who released proper prog-rock albums in 1976 and 1977. Scenes have a tendency to arrive late to Iceland so the albums have a distinctive '1972' air to them. Not taking anything away from the music, which is excellent.
2 Arnar Eggert Thoroddsen, '"Prog Rock? We Can Also Do That!" The Peculiarities of Icelandic Progressive Rock in the 1970s', paper presented at The Progect, Second International Conference on Progressive Rock, University of Edinburgh, 26 May 2016.
3 A rarely used Icelandic word, it can refer to existence or survival. 'Living' – with a double meaning, as both a noun and an adjective – would be a clever translation.
4 Trúbrot now included Magnús Kjartansson from Keflavík, who became one of the most versatile figures in Icelandic music history. As a pianist and keyboard player, he was a member of many of Iceland's most prominent bands, including Haukar, Júdas, Óðmenn, Trúbrot, Mannakorn, Brimkló and Brunaliðið. Magnús has been involved in many different facets of the industry, including record production, arrangements, choir conducting, session playing, songwriting and musician's union work.
5 Dr. Gunni (Gunnar Lárus Hjálmarsson), *Stuð vors lands: Saga dægurtónlistar á Íslandi* (One Jovial Nation: Iceland's Popular Music History) (Reykjavík, 2012), pp. 36–8.
6 Dr. Gunni, *Blue Eyed Pop: The History of Popular Music in Iceland* (Reykjavík, 2013), p. 60. A sale of 5,000 copies constituted gold

in Iceland at this time. However, before 1975 standards were unclear and there are examples of gold records being awarded for sales of 2,500 copies. See the Association of Record Manufacturers website, www.fhf.is (under 'Söluviðurkenningar').

7 Ibid., p. 60.

8 Interestingly, a compilation that covers some of these bands, *Poppsaga: Iceland's Pop Scene, 1972–1977*, was released in 2014 by the British RPM International label. Liner notes written by Dr. Gunni.

9 *Ertu í stuði?* or 'Are you in a jovial mood?/Are you up for it?' is quite a common greeting, not only used at parties and on the dancefloor but in mundane, everyday situations, such as when you are killing time at the office water cooler.

10 A play on words. Geimsteinn is deliberately supposed to bring the word *gimsteinn* to mind, which means diamond. The words sound almost identical in fast speak.

11 See reference 4 above.

12 He also released some countrified albums at the beginning of the 1990s, under the Sléttuúlfarnir moniker (The Coyotes).

13 Gsal, 'Fyrst þarf maður að sigra sjálfan sig – svo heiminn', *Tíminn*, 17 August 1975, pp. 20–21, 27. Gsal was the abbreviated name of pop critic and journalist Gunnar Salvarsson.

14 The term in Icelandic is *að meika það*, which means to 'make it' as a musician, fame and fortune wise. There's also a noun, *meikið* or 'the make'.

15 The album was intended for release by the end of 1975, and the labels on the copies bore that year. However, shipping delays pushed the release date to 4 March 1976. Nonetheless, 1975 is most often cited as the release year on official information sites.

16 arnart@mbl.is, 'Manna sem féll af himnum', *Morgunblaðið*, 21 September 2001, p. 50. The author (that is, this author) is given as an email address because at this time *Morgunblaðið* sometimes used email addresses solely to designate shorter articles.

17 A list of the 100 greatest Icelandic albums of all time was published in a book under the same name in the autumn of 2009, featuring extensive writing on each album by Icelandic pop historian Jónatan Garðarsson and this author. The list itself was compiled in conjunction with key figures from the music business and the general public. Published as *100 bestu plötur Íslandssögunnar* (The 100 Greatest Icelandic Albums of All Time) (Reykjavík, 2009).

18 Dr. Gunni, *Blue Eyed Pop*, p. 71. See also Jón Karl Helgason, 'Burðarvirki íslenskrar nútímamenningar' (The Institutional Pillars

of Modern Icelandic Culture), in *Saga Íslands* (The History of Iceland), 11 vols, ed. Pétur Hrafn Árnason and Sigurður Líndal (Reykjavík, 2016), vol. XI, pp. 319–406.

19 The 'wool sweater' declaration is quoted from Egill Ólafsson (a member of Spilverk þjóðanna and Stuðmenn, as well as the frontman of Hinn íslenzki þursaflokkur) during a conversation with this author in February 2008, outside a nondescript coffee house in downtown Reykjavík.

20 Dr. Gunni, *Blue Eyed Pop*, p. 72.

21 Gestur Guðmundsson, *Rokksaga Íslands: frá Sigga Johnnie til Sykurmolanna* (Iceland's Rock History: From Siggi Johnnie to The Sugarcubes) (Reykjavík, 1990), p. 97.

22 Dr. Gunni, *Blue Eyed Pop*, p. 76.

23 Ibid. Also Gestur Guðmundsson, *Iceland's Rock History*, p. 98.

24 Ómar Valdimarsson, 'Íslensk lýsergíðtónlist', *Morgunblaðið*, 21 June 1975, p. 9.

25 Dr. Gunni, *Jovial Nation*, p. 216.

26 The letters CD correspond to the album sides: A and B on the first record, C and D on this one, and so forth. The last album had sides J and K, while the one before that had I and the Icelandic Í. The fourth album, *Sturla*, did not feature letters on the label or on the cover. *Nærlífi* (or Nearlife) refers to the recording itself, as it was 'nearly live'.

27 *Þokkabót*, in the most common sense, means 'to add insult to injury'. But the literal meaning is 'added beauty or grace', a meaning that the members were going after without a doubt.

28 See Hörður's biography, *Tabú* (Akureyri, 2008). Also *Bylting* (Reykjavík, 2018), where he talks about his involvement in the 'Pots and Pans' revolution. For academic writing, see Jón Gunnar Bernburg, *Economic Crisis and Mass Protest: The Pots and Pans Revolution in Iceland* (Abingdon, 2016).

29 Dr. Gunni, *Blue Eyed Pop*, p. 82.

30 Arnar Eggert Thoroddsen, 'Haldið þið Þursar við!', *Morgunblaðið*, 23 July 2000, p. 14B. Egill also mentioned to this author around the 2007–8 comeback that he would like to try to compose something new with the band, although nothing of that sort has been aired officially.

31 The albums are *Á bleikum náttkjólum* (In Pink Nightgowns) by Spilverk þjóðanna and Megas (number three), the debut album by Þursaflokkurinn (number four), *Sumar á Sýrlandi* by Stuðmenn (number five) and *Sturla* by Spilverk þjóðanna

(number ten). *Ágætis byrjun* by Sigur Rós claims the top spot, followed by *Lifun* by Trúbrot, an album that was perennially at the top in all similar polls right up to the book's publication in 2009.

32 Árni Matthíasson, 'Geimveran Björk', *Morgunblaðið*, 11 November 1990, pp. 12–13C.

33 Well, the nowhere being Norway, where he was studying at the time.

34 Jónatan Garðarsson and Arnar Eggert Thoroddsen, *The 100 Greatest Icelandic Albums of All Time*, p. 35.

35 The perfect band name, considering Megas's emulation of Dylan.

36 The album was the first Icelandic album to make use of a newly installed 24-channel console at Hljóðriti.

37 Arnar Eggert Thoroddsen, 'Vor í Skálholti', *Morgunblaðið*, 12 April 2001, p. 72.

38 þhs, 'Megas skuldar engum neitt', DV, 20 October 2001, p. 23.

39 Egill Ólafsson, 'off-dictaphone' comment to this author after an interview concerning the 2007–8 comeback of Þursaflokkurinn. 'Við vorum ekki að keppa við neitt nema sjálfa okkur', *Morgunblaðið*, 2 February 2008, pp. 4–5.

4 The 1980s: Punk Emerges and The Sugarcubes Break the Chain

1 Excerpt from David Fricke, 'The Sugarcubes: The Coolest Band in the World', *Rolling Stone*, 14 July 1988. It is the first 'something is stirring in Iceland' article of its kind, setting the scene for what was to follow.

2 DIY is an abbreviation for 'do-it-yourself'. In culture, it refers to 'the ethic of self-sufficiency through completing tasks without the aid of a paid expert . . . promoting the idea that anyone is capable of performing a variety of tasks rather than relying on paid specialists'. See for example Amy Spencer, *DIY: The Rise of Lo-Fi Culture* (London, 2005).

3 Other general documentaries about Icelandic pop music are *Popp í Reykjavík* (Pop in Reykjavík, 1998) and *Gargandi snilld* (Screaming Masterpiece, 2005).

4 For further ruminations on this, see Nathan Wiseman-Trowse, *Performing Class in British Popular Music* (London, 2008).

5 Unnur María Bergsveinsdóttir, 'Ekta íslenskt pönk? Myndun íslenskrar pönkmenningar' (Real Icelandic Punk? The Formation of Icelandic Punk Culture), MA thesis, University of Iceland, 2014.

6 As a curious sidenote, punk bypassed the Faroe Islands completely (population 43,000 at the time).

7 Gestur Guðmundsson, *Rokksaga Íslands: frá Sigga Johnnie til Sykurmolanna* (Iceland's Rock History: From Siggi Johnnie to The Sugarcubes) (Reykjavík, 1990), p. 181.

8 This phrase can also be applied to the workings of the Icelandic popular music world at large and Icelandic society in general. *Þetta reddast* has recently entered tourist books as one of Iceland's unique quirks and many Iceland enthusiasts are transfixed by it: 'So frequently used, it has been described as the country's motto' (Sara McMahon, 'What Does "þetta reddast" Mean?', *Iceland Magazine*, www.icelandmag.is, 9 June 2014). It means 'Let's not worry. It will work out somehow,' and, on closer inspection, carries with it an almost Zen-like attitude to life. Because the deeper meaning is, 'It will be OK, even if it does not pan out how you envisioned it.' On the other hand, the phrase, which is usually expressed with an almost careless (yet optimistic) tone, is said to describe well how unorganized Icelanders are, doing everything at the last minute. The attitude that comes with it is really both a blessing and a curse and characterizes the popular music scene in many ways. See also Katie Hammel, 'The Unexpected Philosophy Icelanders Live By', BBC *Travel*, www.bbc.com, 24 April 2020.

9 The non-bureaucratic, informal approach to things that characterizes Icelandic society in many ways tends to be the norm in small-scale societies, see for example Joseph Henrich et al., *Foundations of Human Sociality: Economic Experiments and Ethnographic Evidence from Fifteen Small-Scale Societies* (New York, 2004).

10 According to a 2024 census.

11 Gestur Guðmundsson, *Iceland's Rock History*, p. 197.

12 Dr. Gunni (Gunnar Lárus Hjálmarsson), assisted by Haukur S. Magnússon, *Blue Eyed Pop: The History of Popular Music in Iceland* (Reykjavík, 2013), p. 82. The term *vísa* (*vísnavinir*, *vísnasöngvar*) primarily refers to Scandinavian verse singing, a tradition embraced by Nordic mainstream pop and rock stars in the late 1960s and 1970s, who incorporated it into their music in varying degrees.

13 Ísbjörninn (The Polar Bear) was a fish-freezing plant in the capital area.

14 Tappi Tíkarrass was formed in 1981. This was pure punk pop, which according to the bassist's dad 'fit like a cork in a bitch's ass!'

15 Another nonsense band name. 'Sleepy Chess-Player' has been offered and has made the Internet rounds (but sources are unclear), with Pillnikk referencing chess player Carl Pilnick and Purrkur *svefnpurka*, which means a sleepy person.

16 The scope of the book hinders me from delving thoroughly into the popular music history of the rural Icelandic areas. Some bands and artists get a mention as a part of reporting a scene (the South Iceland pop bands for instance; more of that in the 2000s chapter) but some are left out, unfairly it could be argued in some instances. I will mention three favourites, however. Ljótu hálfvitarnir (Ugly Idiots) from Húsavík, Pogueish jesters and popular live favourites. Geirmundur Valtýsson, 'The King of the Icelandic Swing', hailing from Sauðárkrókur in the northwest. His music is strict 'dansband' music in the vein of Sven-Ingvars (Sweden) and German schlager music. And last but not least, the band Helgi og Hljóðfæraleikararnir (Helgi and the Instrument Players) from Kristnes, a small village just outside of Akureyri. Led by the highly charismatic Helgi Þórsson, the band is made up of brothers and cousins and plays idiosyncratic folk-punk. They are local legends who also enjoy cult adoration around the country.

17 Árni Matthíasson, 'Ási í Faco, Fálkanum, Gramminu, Geisla, Japís og Smekkleysu', *Morgunblaðið Magazine*, 17 April 2005, pp. 12–19.

18 This direct translation of the band's name was found in one of their songs, 'Playing Fool'. The literal meaning is someone who is obsessed by card games.

19 Her highest charting was in 1995 when 'It's Oh So Quiet' made it to number four, a cover of a Betty Hutton B-side, originally released in 1951.

20 Our best Olympic achievement is the silver medal won by triple jumper Vilhjálmur Einarsson in 1956. This accomplishment was matched in 2008 when our handball team secured a silver medal.

21 Their keyboardist, Eyþór Gunnarsson, is one of the most revered musicians in Iceland, recognized for his work as a composer, producer, arranger and performer. He has diverse experience across multiple musical genres and has collaborated with numerous artists, both domestically and internationally.

22 Valur Gunnarsson, 'A Very Brief History of Icelandic Film Making', *Reykjavík Grapevine*, www.grapevine.is, 9 June 2009.

23 *Músíktilraunir* translates literally to 'Music Experiments', a description that falls short in capturing the diverse musical talents showcased in the competition. While some highly experimental bands participate occasionally, the event primarily features teenage bands and musicians, offering a glimpse into the vibrant music scene brewing in Iceland's garages and bedrooms. People 'experimenting',

as in taking their first tentative steps rather than writing and playing experimental music.

24 Arnar Eggert Thoroddsen, ‘Nurturing the Roots: Músíktilraunir, Iceland’s Foremost “Battle of the Bands” Competition’, in *Sounds Icelandic: Essays on Icelandic Music in the 20th and 21st Centuries*, ed. Þorbjörg Daphne Hall et al. (Sheffield, 2018), pp. 101–13.

25 A play on words, *Útrás* literally means ‘out-channel’ but the meaning is to ‘vent’ or ‘blow off steam’; *Útvarp Rót* means ‘Radio Root’.

26 Pax Vobis’s singer, Geiri Sæm, went on to enjoy a healthy career as a pop singer at the end of the 1980s/start of the 1990s, with an ambitious pop music derived from Lloyd Cole, Prefab Sprout, David Sylvian and the like.

27 Rúnar, a guitarist skilled in both classical and rock music, would later release contemplative, progressive solo albums, and Rafn, while he lived, was a charismatic force, making and producing music and running a label. He died in 2004 after a long battle with motor neurone disease.

28 Helgi Jónsson, ‘Grafík’, *Glatkistan*, www.glatkistan.com, 9 April 2020.

29 Later, at the start of the 1990s, the town would be known as the ‘heavy rock capital’ of Iceland, as far removed as possible from the light-hearted fun-pop that Greifarnir rolled out in the 1980s. This author visited the town in the late 1990s, went into a bookstore, and the only music magazines he found were *Metal Hammer* and *Kerrang!* Today, the town is also bound up with the film *Eurovision Song Contest: The Story of Fire Saga* (2020), starring Will Ferrell and Rachel McAdams.

30 The influence of Bad Taste has been a widely discussed topic among academics in Iceland, with several BA and MA theses dedicated to it.

31 The original proclamation goes: ‘Það er ekki hvað þú *getur* heldur hvað þú *gerir*!’

32 Excerpts from the manifesto can be found at www.smekkleysa.net (under ‘Our History’), accessed 3 April 2025.

33 Árni Matthíasson, *Sykurmolarnir* (The Sugarcubes) (Reykjavík, 1992), p. 36.

34 Arnar Eggert Thoroddsen, ‘Sykurmolarnir – Life’s Too Good’, in *1001 Albums You Must Hear Before You Die*, ed. Robert Dimery (London, 2005), p. 601.

35 Árni Matthíasson, *The Sugarcubes*, p. 23; Árni Matthíasson, ‘Við þurfum svigrúm til að vera við sjálf’, *Morgunblaðið*, 18 October 1987, p. 28.

36 'The soul of my John' is a reference to a well-known Icelandic play, while 'New Danish' references a common window ad in Icelandic bookstores when new Danish magazines had arrived.

37 A status that was further solidified during the COVID-19 pandemic when a streamed concert series with him as a host was a sensational success.

5 The 1990s: The World Domination of Björk

1 The band won under the Infusoria moniker, apparently because the name was more 'commercial'. It was quickly changed back.

2 A simple critical assessment from this author after a lifetime of observing these scenes.

3 *Gerningaveður* literally means weather that's besotted by an evil spell.

4 Rumour has it that Eiríkur was at one time considered as a vocalist for Iron Maiden after Bruce Dickinson's departure in 1993.

5 A highly interesting artefact was released in 1987 by the mysterious band Flames of Hell. The album, *Fire and Steel*, contains weird and wonderful proto-black metal music and is a highly sought-after collector's item.

6 Dr. Gunni (Gunnar Lárus Hjálmarsson), *Stuð vors lands: Saga dægurtónlistar á Íslandi* (One Jovial Nation: Iceland's Popular Music History) (Reykjavík, 2012), p. 249.

7 Released only on CD, as vinyl releases ceased in 1991 and did not fully resurface again until the 2010s.

8 Kolrassa krókríðandi is a woman's name from an Icelandic folktale.

9 Named after the graphic novel by American cartoonist Art Spiegelman. The word *Maus* is German for 'mouse' (pronounced *maʊ̯s*). Icelandic youth, most of it unfamiliar with the novel (or German for that matter), pronounced it as *mœys*. The band eventually embraced this pronunciation as it coincidentally aligns with an old Icelandic word. As a noun it means something bothersome and effortful to see through, while as a verb it signifies dabbling with something in a relatively carefree manner.

10 The biggest loss is the magnificent SSSpan, an aggro-rock band that operated for a few months in 1993, playing legendary gigs. The music was a pummelling take on U.S. underground heroes like The Jesus Lizard and Big Black and it's still ringing in our ears all these years later but unfortunately nowhere else.

11 Jónatan Garðarsson and Arnar Eggert Thoroddsen, *100 bestu plötur Íslandssögunnar* (The 100 Greatest Icelandic Albums of All Time) (Reykjavík, 2009), p. 202.

12 His apprentice of sorts, Árni Grétar Jóhannesson, carried the electronic torch from the 2000s onwards. As Futuregrapher, he released dozens of records in various styles, with ambient and techno being the most eminent. He was a co-founder of Möller Records, one of Iceland's main electronic music labels, and through his own label, Móatún 7, he released hundreds of records by domestic and international artists. He sadly passed away prematurely in 2025, just like his mentor, Biogen, who died in 2011.

13 One of the longest-running radio shows in Iceland is *Party Zone*, a dance/electronica show; techno, house and related electronic music genres have long been a part of Icelandic music culture, primarily thriving underground.

14 Kristín Björk Kristjánsdóttir, 'Hljóðbúningur í Tilraunaeldhúsinu', *Morgunblaðið*, 1 May 1999, p. 88.

15 For a brief time the collective had a fourth member, Pétur Hallgrímsson (Lhooq).

16 Arnar Eggert Thoroddsen, 'Orgelstuð og útvarpsfikt', *Morgunblaðið*, 28 September 2000, p. 58; Úlfur Eldjárn, one of the members, has an impressive solo career where he writes music for films, television, the stage and his own experimental projects.

17 Árni Matthíasson, 'Íslenski rokkdraumurinn', *Morgunblaðið*, 10 January 1999, pp. 10–11.

18 Nick Prior, '"It's A Social Thing, Not a Nature Thing": Popular Music Practices in Reykjavík, Iceland', *Cultural Sociology*, IX/1 (2015), pp. 81–98 (p. 92).

19 The album was part of the *Trumpet Series* (*Lúðraserían*), which contained eight records that showcased the best underground bands at the time. Sigur Rós effectively broke the record label bank with this record as the studio budget far exceeded the allotted label limit.

20 Arnar Eggert Thoroddsen, 'Sigur Rós – Ágætis byrjun', in *1001 Albums You Must Hear Before You Die*, ed. Robert Dimery (London, 2005), p. 857.

21 Ian Watson, 'Sigur Ros – Stunningly Beautiful Soundscapes', *Melody Maker*, LXXVI/45 (10 November 1999), p. 10.

22 Margrét S. Sigurðardóttir and Tómas Young, *Towards Creative Iceland: Building Local, Going Global – Quantitative and Qualitative Mapping of the Cultural and Creative Sectors in Iceland* (Reykjavík, 2011), report for Íslandsstofa (Business Iceland).

23 Other important festivals are, for example, Extreme Chill Festival, which has been going since 2009, offering all kinds of experimental music, and is run by the passionate underground scenester and

musician Pan Thorarensen; Aldrei fór ég suður (I Never Ventured South), a comfy but exotic music festival in the Westfjords; and Innipúkinn (The Homebody), a Reykjavík festival for those who can't bear to go camping come the Icelandic Bank holiday. All kinds of festivals have come and gone through the decades, of course, and what I've detailed is by no means comprehensive.

6 The 2000s: Sigur Rós and the Icelandic Popular Music Phenomenon

1 Arnar Eggert Thoroddsen, 'Friðarstund', *Morgunblaðið*, 25 October 2000, p. 55.

2 The quartet started to release its own music in 2004. Incorporating elements of contemporary classical compositions and electronic loops, the band played a prominent role in the ethereal, avant-garde wave that resonated internationally in the 2000s. Another notable band in a similar vein is Rökkurró, which released two fine albums through the 12 Tónar record label in 2007 and 2010.

3 The track that this author named 'The organ song' in his Reykjavík Free Church review.

4 Jónatan Garðarsson and Arnar Eggert Thoroddsen, *100 bestu plötur Íslandssögunnar* (The 100 Greatest Icelandic Albums of All Time) (Reykjavík, 2009), p. 20.

5 Sharon O'Connell, 'Heima', *Time Out*, www.timeout.com, 29 October 2007.

6 Jónatan Garðarsson and Arnar Eggert Thoroddsen, *100 Greatest Icelandic Albums*, p. 154.

7 Ibid.

8 Arnar Eggert Thoroddsen, 'Innlit í undraheim', *Morgunblaðið*, 31 August 2004, p. 38.

9 Arnar Eggert Thoroddsen, 'Leaves', *Morgunblaðið*, 24 March 2007, pp. 54–5.

10 Jón is one of Iceland's most industrious music figures, serving as a producer, radio personality, TV host, managing director of FTT (ISAC, the Icelandic Society of Authors and Composers), label owner and one-time distributor through jon.is, one of Iceland's earliest music websites. He actively writes and performs music both with Nýdönsk and as a solo artist.

11 Jónatan Garðarsson and Arnar Eggert Thoroddsen, *100 Greatest Icelandic Albums*, p. 118.

12 Guðni Rúnar Gunnarsson, the lead singer of Klink, later formed the notorious duo Dr. Mister & Mr. Handsome with Ívar Örn

Kolbeinsson. Their debut album, *Dirty Slutty Hooker Money*, was released in 2006.

13 'Subculture affiliated with the hardcore punk scene, followers of which abstain from alcohol, tobacco, recreational drugs, and "promiscuous" sex. Some also abstain from caffeine or follow a vegan or vegetarian diet.' Emily Kendall, 'Straight Edge', *Britannica*, www.britannica.com, accessed 1 October 2024.

14 A theory has been put forward about a wave that could be placed between these two ('Wave 1.5') and pop rap groups such as Igore have been mentioned as well as Dabbi T and Poetrix (who released albums in 2008). However, all these examples are specific, there was no scene as such and Icelandic hip-hop was pretty much underground at this time.

15 Named as such because the band was a thrash band when it originally started out.

16 Comeback concerts with said bands, happening at the time of writing, are dubbed 'millennial concerts'.

17 Arnar Eggert Thoroddsen, *Umboðsmaður Íslands: Öll trixin í bókinni* (Iceland's Svengali: All the Tricks in the Book) (Reykjavík, 2007).

18 Arnar Eggert Thoroddsen, 'Einar Bárðarson', in *Hressilegt athafnafólk* (Movers and Shakers), ed. Karl Helgason (Reykjavík, 2007), pp. 74–90.

19 See www.icelandmusic.is. Here are some key points from its 'manifesto': 'Iceland Music will provide both education and support to musicians and music-related companies, support the development of the music industry, promote Icelandic music and musicians abroad, and serve as a distributor for Icelandic compositions . . . With the establishment of the Music Center, a significant step is taken towards giving the art form greater importance and providing a clear path for Icelandic musicians, both domestically and internationally.' A precursor to Iceland Music was the Icelandic Music Export Office, founded in 2006. It took initial steps to support and regulate the Icelandic music industry, particularly concerning foreign export efforts.

20 As told to the author by Guðm. Kristinn Jónsson.

21 To paint a somewhat romantic picture, two of the Swedes resided in a boathouse for a while. Unfortunately, it was equipped with a DVD player and a surround sound system, which ruins my feeble attempt at a starving artists' tale.

22 The phrase references Elvis's hoodlums but also draws from a humorous line by Björgvin Halldórsson. Bo, the Icelandic 'Elvis',

had an office in the same building as the studio. When Kiddi, the main producer and captain, moved in, Bo asked him, 'So, are you coming to Memphis?' Arnar Eggert Thoroddsen, 'Töframaðurinn í Trönuhrauni,' *Morgunblaðið*, 13 May 2007, p. 74.

23 Jónatan Garðarsson and Arnar Eggert Thoroddsen, *100 Greatest Icelandic Albums*, pp. 17, 34, 65 and 110.

24 Ibid., p. 53.

25 Pétur is a respected artist in his own right; he is a renowned producer, solo artist and film composer.

26 Jónatan Garðarsson and Arnar Eggert Thoroddsen, *100 Greatest Icelandic Albums*, p. 53.

27 *Mugiboogie* was about capturing the 'feeling'; one or two wrong notes in the heat of the moment were more welcome than icy technical perfection. The opening track is thus gritty boogie-rock and, to get into the mood, Mugison and the band indulged in a massive BBQ, drank a beer or ten and rocked out late into the night. The morning after, it was time to record. A musical 'method acting' of sorts. Ibid., p. 111.

28 Arnar Eggert Thoroddsen, 'Hr. Gott blóð', *Morgunblaðið*, 29 September 2011, p. 35.

29 Mugison has kept busy to this day with regular concerts. His latest venture (2024) is playing in one hundred churches in one hundred postal codes in a single year.

30 Arnar Eggert Thoroddsen, 'Music-Making in a Northern Isle: Iceland and the "Village" Factor', PhD thesis, University of Edinburgh, 2019.

31 In a BA thesis I supervised for the Iceland University of the Arts, a case is made that pure Icelandic folk simply reminds Icelanders too much of their horrible past as a colony. The music – embedded in a generational trauma of sorts – thus brings back painful memories of poverty and hardship. That's the reason why it has never been fully embraced by the masses or the musicians, apart from the examples detailed in the book. Bjarni Karlsson, 'Íslensk þjóðlagatónlist – Dauði og upprisa' ('Icelandic Folk Music – Death and Resurrection'), BA thesis, Iceland University of the Arts, 2024.

32 A video of the band went viral when they performed an eight-hundred-year-old Icelandic hymn in an impromptu fashion at a German train station. The video has 8 million views at the time of writing. The hymn, 'Heyr, himna smiður', was written by the powerful Icelandic chieftain Kolbeinn Tumason in 1208 on his deathbed. The music was composed in the 1970s by Þorkell Sigurbjörnsson (1938–2013), one of Iceland's foremost contemporary composers.

33 Another weighty electro band around that time was Bloodgroup, formed by Faroe Islander Janus Rasmussen and the siblings Ragnar Jónsson, Lilja Jónsdóttir and Hallur Jónsson. The same can be said about AmPop, who had a good run, commercially and artistically, this decade as did Sykur (Sugar), with the indomitable Agnes Björt in the front.

34 Arnar Eggert Thoroddsen, 'Nýir tímar', *Morgunblaðið*, 23 November 2009, p. 26.

35 Arnar Eggert Thoroddsen, 'Krossferðinni lokið', *Morgunblaðið*, 6 February 2008, p. 32.

36 Andie Sophia Fontaine, 'Off the Rails with Grísalappalísa: The Iconic Band Bids Adieu', *Reykjavík Grapevine*, www.grapevine.is, 25 October 2019.

37 I also mention Biggi Hilmars and Herdís Stefánsdóttir as important names in this 'scene'.

38 Michael Nordine, '"Blade Runner 2049" Soundtrack: Denis Villeneuve Finally Reveals Why Jóhann Jóhannsson Left the Project', *IndieWire*, www.indiewire.com, 30 September 2017.

39 From the 'About' section on www.bedroomcommunity.net, accessed 3 April 2025.

40 Andie Sophia Fontaine, 'The View from the Piano: Damon Albarn's Love Affair with Iceland', *Reykjavík Grapevine*, www.grapevine.is, 5 November 2021.

41 Former GusGus member President Bongo has made a notable impact this decade as a solo artist, primarily through his ambitious project Les Aventures De President Bongo, which aims for a total of 24 releases. The works include his own music and music by other artists, with the president serving as a curator.

7 The 2010s: An Ever-Growing Interest

1 Arnar Eggert Thoroddsen, 'Lífsblóðið, tónlistin, er alltaf í forgangi', *Morgunblaðið*, 21 September 2011, p. 40.

2 Arnar Eggert Thoroddsen, 'Koma svo, allir saman nú . . .', *Morgunblaðið*, 22 September 2011, p. 37.

3 KEXP has recorded hundreds of sessions at Iceland Airwaves and all of them are available on YouTube.

4 The track 'Little Talks' had been streamed 1 billion times on Spotify when this manuscript was completed (June 2024).

5 The author conducts a tourist walk called the Reykjavík Music Walk and when the tale of OMAM is told, few of the guests realize that the band is Icelandic.

6 Hallur Már, 'Ótrúlegur árangur Of Monsters and Men', *Morgunblaðið* (online video report), www.mbl.is, 5 June 2012.
7 Ibid.
8 And just to reify the Icelandic 'village' factor yet again: the lead singer lives on the same street as this author, a fairly normal pedestrian street near Reykjavík's city centre.
9 *Sátt* means conciliation. The album was released in English and in Icelandic.
10 Confusingly, there is the long-running Nordic Council Music Prize and then the Nordic Music Prize, initiated by the Norwegian by:Larm festival in 2010. The latter price is now defunct.
11 Davíð Ólafsson and Arnar Eggert Thoroddsen, 'Plundering on Sacred Ground: The Viking Rock of Iceland's Skálmöld and Its Bid to "High" Culture', unpublished, draft article.
12 As quoted by Snæbjörn Ragnarsson, a member of Skálmöld, to the author in March 2016.
13 Or some goddess from Norse mythology!
14 An Icelandic word for the 'radiating sunbeams' phenomenon.
15 Arnar Eggert Thoroddsen, 'Frostköld fegurð', *Morgunblaðið*, 19 March 2009, p. 43.
16 Arnar Eggert Thoroddsen, 'Spáð er vaxandi stormviðri af norðri', *Morgunblaðið*, 27 October 2011, p. 34.
17 *Ótta* is an old Icelandic appellation for the time from 3 a.m. to 6 a.m.
18 Arnar Eggert Thoroddsen, 'Þegar allt varð svart', *Morgunblaðið*, 12 December 2015, p. 105.
19 The heavy/extreme metal festival scene has been thriving, with four to five festivals taking place every year, sometimes more. For a long time, the Eistnaflug (Flight of the Testicles) festival in the Eastfjords (Neskaupsstaður) was the main event but it came to an end a few years ago. The Sátan festival in Stykkishólmur has now taken up the mantle, holding its inaugural event in the summer of 2024. Other festivals like ReykjaDoom, Andkristnihátíð, Ascencion, Norðanpaunk and Reykjavík Deathfest cater to different genres, although the criteria for inclusion is often quite flexible due to the circumstances of being a micronation.
20 Arnar Eggert Thoroddsen, 'Rýmið er lítið en hjartað er stórt', *Morgunblaðið*, 18 May 2019, p. 53.
21 Arnar Eggert Thoroddsen, 'Makt myrkursins', *Morgunblaðið*, 23 July 2016, p. 49.
22 Arnar Eggert Thoroddsen, 'Dýpra og dýpra', *Morgunblaðið*, 6 November 2021, p. 50.

23 Arnar Eggert Thoroddsen, 'Óræð fegurð', *Morgunblaðið*, 24 August 2010, p. 30.

24 See 'Sóley Stefánsdóttir', *Nordic Co-Operation*, www.norden.org, accessed 23 January 2025. A rationale text for the Nordic Council Music Prize, written by this author.

25 Arnar Eggert Thoroddsen, 'Társtokkið teiti', *Morgunblaðið*, 22 February 2020, p. 43.

26 Davíð Þór Jónsson stepped up in the early 2000s as one of Iceland's most promising jazz prodigies, leading a change in tact and emphasis that the new jazz generation brought with it. A versatile artist, equally skilled in piano playing, composition and conducting orchestras, he has composed music and soundtracks for numerous performances, radio plays, television programmes and dance performances. He has also collaborated closely with stage artists and visual artists. See 'Davíð Þór Jónsson bæjarlistamaður Mosfellsbæjar 2017', *Mosfellingur*, www.mosfellingur.is, 29 August 2017. Another important figure rising from the 2000s jazz upheavals, if we can say so, is one Samúel J. Samúelsson, an ever-constant presence in brass arranging, playing, conducting, bridging genres and preaching 'the funk', for example with his band Jagúar.

27 Arnar Eggert Thoroddsen, 'Lokkandi stef á lygnum værðarsjó', RÚV, www.ruv.is, 17 June 2017.

28 Arnar Eggert Thoroddsen, 'Rökkurópera Valdimars', RÚV, www.ruv.is, 29 September 2018.

29 Pétur Magnússon, 'Dikta í tuttugu ár', *Morgunblaðið* (Sunday edition), 9 June 2019, p. 10.

30 Arnar Eggert Thoroddsen, 'Óbærilegur léttleiki tilverunnar', RÚV, www.ruv.is, 28 April 2018.

31 Kristján Eldjárn also comes to mind, a virtuoso guitarist proficient in classical guitar, blues and pop/rock styles. He managed to make a big impact on the Icelandic music scene at large during his lifetime. He passed away from cancer at the age of 29 in 2002.

32 Arnar Eggert Thoroddsen, 'Harpa, hysjaðu upp um þig', *Morgunblaðið*, 10 June 2011, p. 39.

33 Arnar Eggert Thoroddsen, 'Allt galopið', *Morgunblaðið*, 31 August 2019, p. 43.

34 Post-dreifing upload their releases on the Bandcamp platform. This platform has facilitated a marked increase in Icelandic music releases overall, especially in the last five years. The music naturally varies in quality, but this shift away from traditional distribution

methods, seen worldwide with various streaming platforms, has certainly been felt here as well as elsewhere.

35 Two BA theses have been written about the collective. See also Michael P. Farrell, *Collaborative Circles: Friendship Dynamics and Creative Work* (Chicago, IL, 2001).

36 Nick Prior, '"It's A Social Thing, Not a Nature Thing": Popular Music Practices in Reykjavík, Iceland', *Cultural Sociology*, IX/1 (2015), pp. 81–98 (p. 93).

37 Think Cafe OTO in London.

38 Arnar Eggert Thoroddsen, 'Hugsað um Hatara', *Morgunblaðið*, 8 June 2019, p. 44.

39 I took to my Facebook page (on 4 July 2020) and wrote some thoughts about the film, and the comments section was lively to say the least.

8 The 2020s: Where to Next?

1 The latter often accompanied by her husband, Guðmundur Pétursson (Gummi P), one of Iceland's best-known virtuoso guitarists.

2 Biographical information compiled from text on the Mengi website, www.mengi.net, accessed 3 April 2025.

3 The term was coined in the mid-1990s by Irwin Chusid. A short but well-referenced Wikipedia page gives this explanation: 'Outsider music (from "outsider art") is music created by self-taught or naïve musicians. The term is usually applied to musicians who have little or no traditional musical experience, who exhibit childlike qualities in their music, or who have intellectual disabilities or mental illnesses.' I'm well aware of the pitfalls of Wikipedia as a reliable source but the relevant references have been thoroughly tried and tested by the author. See also Adam Harper, 'Lo-Fi Aesthetics in Popular Music Discourse', DPhil thesis, University of Oxford, 2014; Árni Hjörvar Árnason, '"Bein útsending úr brjóstkassanum": Einfarar í íslenskri tónlist' ('Straight from the Heart': Icelandic Outsider Musicians), BA thesis, University of Iceland, 2023; and Irwin Chusid, *Songs in the Key of Z: The Curious Universe of Outsider Music* (Chicago, IL, 2000).

Conclusion: Why Iceland?

1 Nick Prior, '"It's A Social Thing, Not a Nature Thing": Popular Music Practices in Reykjavík, Iceland', *Cultural Sociology*, IX/1 (2015), pp. 81–98 (p. 93).

2 See ibid., for example, for an academic observation regarding this characteristic of Icelandic music culture, but also Tore Størvold, *Dissonant Landscapes: Music, Nature, and the Performance of Iceland* (Middletown, CT, 2023) and Joshua Green, *Music-Making in the Faroes: The Experience of Music-Making in the Faroes and Making Metal Faroese* (Vestmanna, 2013).

3 The talk/session was titled 'On the Value of Popular Music', held 26 May 2017.

4 Ruth Finnegan, *The Hidden Musicians: Music-Making in an English Town* (Cambridge, 1989), pp. 324–5. My emphasis.

Select Discography

1950s

Various Artists, *Aftur til fortíðar '50–'60* (compilation, 1990)
Various Artists, *Aftur til fortíðar '50–'60, annar hluti* (compilation, 1991)
Various Artists, *Aftur til fortíðar '50–'60, þriðji hluti* (compilation, 1991)
Erla Þorsteinsdóttir, *Stúlkan með lævirkjaröddina* (compilation, 2000)
Haukur Morthens, *Ó borg mín borg* (compilation, 2000)
Ragnar Bjarnason, *Þannig týnist tíminn: Vinsælustu lög Ragga Bjarna* (compilation, 2020)

1960s

Savanna Trio, *Folksongs from Iceland* (1964)
Dátar, *Dátar*, EP (1966)
Elly Vilhjálms, *Lög úr söngleikjum og kvikmyndum* (1966)
Dátar, *Dátar*, EP (1967)
Hljómar, *Hljómar* (1967)
Hljómar, *Hljómar II* (1968)
Ríó tríó, 'Ríó tríó', EP (1968)
Trúbrot, *Trúbrot* (1969)
Thor's Hammer, *From Keflavík,... with love* (compilation, 2001)

1970s

Óðmenn, *Óðmenn* (1970)
Trúbrot, *Lifun* (1971)
Náttúra, *Magic Key* (1972)
Change, *Change* (1974)
Mannakorn, *Mannakorn* (1975)
Stuðmenn, *Sumar á Sýrlandi* (1975)
Megas, *Fram og aftur blindgötuna* (1976)
Spilverk þjóðanna, *Sturla* (1977)
Vilhjálmur Vilhjálmsson, *Hana-nú* (1977)

Hinn íslenzki þursaflokkur, *Hinn íslenzki þursaflokkur* (1978)
Brimkló, *Sígildar sögur með Brimkló* (compilation, 1996)

1980s

Utangarðsmenn, Geislavirkir (1980)
Purrkur Pillnikk, *Ekki enn (aka EhgjI En:)* (1981) (the original release had the album name and the song names phonetically transcribed on the cover. The normal spelling, *Ekki enn*, is used almost exclusively today)
Þeyr, *Mjötviður Mær* (1981)
Mezzoforte, *Surprise Surprise* (1982)
Grýlurnar, *Mávastellið* (1983)
Dúkkulísur, *Dúkkulísur* (1984)
Bubbi Morthens, *Kona* (1985)
Rikshaw, *Rikshaw*, EP (1985)
Bjartmar Guðlaugsson, *Í fylgd með fullorðnum* (1987)
S.H. Draumur, *Goð* (1987)
Síðan skein sól, *Síðan skein sól* (1988)
The Sugarcubes, *Life's Too Good* (1988)

1990s

Todmobile, *Todmobile* (1990)
Nýdönsk, *Deluxe* (1991)
Sálin hans Jóns míns, *Sálin hans Jóns míns* (1991)
KK Band, *Bein leið* (1992)
Kolrassa Krókríðandi, *Drápa* (1992)
Björk, *Debut* (1993)
Páll Óskar, *Stuð* (1993)
GusGus, *GusGus* (1995)
Maus, *Lof mér að falla að þínu eyra* (1997)
Botnleðja, *Magnyl* (1998)
Emilíana Torrini, *Love in the Time of Science* (1999)
Sigur Rós, *Ágætis byrjun* (1999)
Skítamórall, *Skítamórall* (1999)

2000s

XXX Rottweilerhundar, *XXX Rottweilerhundar* (2001)
Jóhann Jóhannsson, *Englabörn* (2002)
Leaves, *Breathe* (2002)
múm, *Finally We Are No One* (2002)
Quarashi, *Jinx* (2002)

Mínus, *Halldór Laxness* (2003)
Hjálmar, *Hjálmar* (2005)
Lay Low, *Please Don't Hate Me* (2006)
Ólöf Arnalds, *Við og við* (2007)
Hjaltalín, *Terminal* (2009)

2010s

Jónas Sigurðsson, *Allt er eitthvað* (2010)
Skálmöld, *Baldur* (2010)
HAM, *Svik, harmur og dauði* (2011)
Mugison, *Haglél* (2011)
Of Monsters and Men, *My Head Is An Animal* (2011)
Sólstafir, *Svartir sandar* (2011)
Ásgeir Trausti, *Dýrð í dauðaþögn* (2012)
Gísli Pálmi, *Gísli Pálmi* (2015)
Kristín Anna, *Howl* (2015)
Misþyrming, *Söngvar elds og óreiðu* (2015)
JóiPé x Króli, *Gerviglingur* (2017)
Prins Póló, *Þriðja kryddið* (2018)

2020s

Gróa, *What I Like to Do* (2021)
Kælan Mikla, *Undir köldum norðurljósum* (2021)
Sóley, *Mother Melancholia* (2021)
Árný Margrét, *They Only Talk About the Weather* (2022)
Vök, *Vök* (2022)
Daði Freyr, *I Made an Album* (2023)
Laufey, *Bewitched* (2023)

Photo Acknowledgements

The authors and publishers wish to express their thanks to the sources listed below for illustrative material and/or permission to reproduce it:

© Alda: p. 119; © Magnús Anderson: p. 132; © Móheiður Hlíf Geirlaugsdóttir: pp. 53, 160; © Einar Falur Ingólfsson: p. 68; © Rune Kongsro: p. 136; © Eva Mueller: p. 95; © múm: p. 111; promotional material: pp. 19, 22, 23, 28, 31, 36, 50, 56, 61, 67, 70, 75, 84, 86, 102, 108, 114, 116, 121, 122, 126, 137, 143, 145, 151, 154, 157, 167; © Ragnar Th. Sigurðsson: p. 46; © Sony Music Iceland: p. 165; Wikimedia Commons: pp. 80 (Paul Cox/Distributed by Elektra Records/ Public Domain), 162 (Tomzorz/CC BY-SA 4.0).

Index

Page numbers in *italics* refer to illustrations